BUSINESS
LUNCHATATIONS

BUSINESS
LUNCHATATIONS

How an Everyday Guy Became One of

America's Most Powerful CEOs . . .

and How You Can, Too!

 **Bo Dietl**
with Robert W. Bly

Chamberlain Bros.
a member of
Penguin Group (USA) Inc.
New York
2005

CHAMBERLAIN BROS.
Published by the Penguin Group
Penguin Group (USA) Inc., 375 Hudson Street, New York, New York 10014, USA
Penguin Group (Canada), 10 Alcorn Avenue, Toronto, Ontario M4V 3B2, Canada
(a division of Pearson Penguin Canada Inc.)
Penguin Books Ltd, 80 Strand, London WC2R 0RL, England
Penguin Ireland, 25 St Stephen's Green, Dublin 2, Ireland
(a division of Penguin Books Ltd)
Penguin Group (Australia), 250 Camberwell Road, Camberwell, Victoria 3124,
Australia (a division of Pearson Australia Group Pty Ltd)
Penguin Books India Pvt Ltd, 11 Community Centre, Panchsheel Park,
New Delhi–110 017, India
Penguin Group (NZ), Cnr Airborne and Rosedale Roads, Albany, Auckland 1310,
New Zealand (a division of Pearson New Zealand Ltd)
Penguin Books (South Africa) (Pty) Ltd, 24 Sturdee Avenue, Rosebank,
Johannesburg 2196, South Africa

Penguin Books Ltd, Registered Offices: 80 Strand, London WC2R 0RL, England

An application has been submitted to register this book with the Library of Congress.

ISBN 1-59609-053-7

Printed in the United States of America
10 9 8 7 6 5 4 3 2

Book design by Jaime Putorti

This publication is designed to provide accurate and authoritative information in
regard to the subject matter covered. It is sold with the understanding that the publisher is not engaged in rendering legal, accounting, or other professional services.
If you require legal advice or other expert assistance, you should seek the services of
a competent professional.

While the author has made every effort to provide accurate telephone numbers and
Internet addresses at the time of publication, neither the publisher nor the author
assumes any responsibility for errors, or for changes that occur after publication.
Further, the publisher does not have any control over and does not assume any re-
sponsiblilty for author or third-party Web sites or their content.

All photographs are from the author's collection.

To my mother, who thankfully is still alive. We made it through a very tough year and it is your encouragement that keeps me driven.

To my brothers, sister, and most important, my children—Jaclyn, Richard, Dana, and Beau

Some people have only as many friends as the five fingers on their hand. I am extremely lucky to have many dear friends: Steven Witkoff, Sheldon Brody, Danny DelGiorno, Charlie Cumella, Al Weiler, Matt Adell, Ally Salerno, Mike the Russian, Mark Arzoomanian, Imus, Joe Grano, John Myers, Mel Weiss, Ronnie Streppone, Sy Stewart . . . this book is for all you guys, and all of my other close friends.

—Bo Dietl

For my sons, Alex and Stephen, the two most important achievements of my life

—Bob Bly

Acknowledgments

Thanks to our editors, Carlo DeVito and Ron Martirano, for having faith in us and in this book, and to my literary agent, Bob Diforio, for helping to bring us all together on this project.

Thanks also to Ilise Benun for permission to reprint her networking tips in Chapter Three.

Contents

CONTENTS

Introduction

"[Bo Dietl's] credentials as both a public servant and private businessman stand as a towering landmark to all that can be achieved by a man with energy and the courage to believe in himself."

—*EGO* MAGAZINE

"Until his retirement at age thirty-five, Bo Dietl was probably the best detective in New York, having received more than sixty-two Police Department medals and awards and dozens of public-service and community awards."

—*NEW YORK* MAGAZINE

"The Bo Show: it runs nearly round-the-clock in New York, starring professional character Bo Dietl in a variety of roles—detective, bon vivant, radio pundit, sharp

dresser, movie actor. But before he achieved maximum
Bo-ness, he had a legendary career in the NYPD."
—*GQ* MAGAZINE

"Bo Dietl's a pretty fearless guy who speaks his mind."
—STEPHEN BALDWIN

"He's the real thing. I admire him because he's a cop
who has done well."
—RAYMOND KELLY,
NEW YORK CITY POLICE COMMISSIONER

There are some people who radiate success—and others who are
actually successful.

Bo Dietl is both, and in this book, he will show how you can
apply his success principles to achieve incredible results in your
business, your career, even your relationships.

When you meet this former NYC police detective turned
mega-successful corporate CEO, you instantly understand that he
is tough indeed: his physical presence, his management style, his
commanding personality, his work and personal ethics. An article in *Ego* magazine proclaims: "In the city that never sleeps, Bo
Dietl is the Big Apple's no-BS real deal." Bo says, "I like to live life
at 150 miles an hour." But on top of all that, he is an extremely
nice guy, too—fiercely loyal to his friends and willing to do whatever it takes to help them when they need it.

Being strong, tough, and confident has contributed greatly to the extraordinary business, career, and financial success of this former cop, now a self-made multimillionaire entrepreneur and business leader.

During his sixteen years as a Manhattan street cop and detective, Bo Dietl made thousands of felony arrests and solved some of New York City's most notorious cases, including the "Palm Sunday Massacre" murders. His exploits were brought to the big screen in the motion picture *One Tough Cop*, starring Stephen Baldwin as Bo, based on his autobiography.

In 1985, Bo suffered an injury (he hurt his ankle in a skydiving accident) that would have required him to take a desk job—a position to which he was wholly unsuited—and so he retired from the force. At that time, he was earning $30,000 a year—a base salary of $26,000 as a third-grade detective, plus another $4,000 a year in overtime.

"The money was tough," says Bo. "Every cop I knew had to have a second job. I had two kids at the time, ages five and seven, and my take-home was $623 in a paycheck every other week. I just couldn't make ends meet."

That same year, Bo began his career in the private sector rather humbly—as a solo licensed private investigator working out of his home in Queens. Today, he is chairman and CEO of Beau Dietl & Associates (BDA), one of the largest and most successful international security firms in the world, which boasts opulent quarters in midtown Manhattan.

His clients include celebrities such as Charlton Heston, Paul Simon, and Richard Pryor; he has worked with political conventions, the New York Stock Exchange, and foreign dignitaries such as the royal family of Saudi Arabia and countries such as the People's Republic of China.

Most of BDA's work is in corporate security, doing investigations for major corporations such as Mutual of America, Coca-Cola, PaineWebber, Bear Stearns, Sony, Insignia Financial Group, Pitney Bowes, and Lehman Brothers.

Bo has also made tens of millions of dollars as a cofounder, investor, or partner in a dozen other business ventures, including software, data storage, motion pictures, fire-safety products, water purifiers, security technology, lighting systems, and nutritional supplements.

One of Bo's companies, the Voyant Corporation, is an online vision-care portal that provides consumers with a patented online vision test that diagnoses the corrective lenses the consumer needs. Using this prescription information and their digital image, customers can then shop for eyeglass frames and order finished glasses over the Internet.

Bo has a fondness for technology businesses. Another of his companies, Security Solutions, has amassed a team of renowned security experts to provide computer-network security for clients ranging from large multinational corporations to small businesses.

In a partnership he formed with a hologram company, Bo offered a high-tech tracking service for apparel manufacturers who wanted to stop theft of their goods. Like a radio frequency identification chip, the holograms—which contain data about the product's point of origin, distribution route, and intended market—are placed inside clothing labels. By tracking the holograms, the manufacturer can detect when shipments are purloined.

But here's the amazing thing: Most of the principles that led to Bo's success—the mental and physical toughness, the commanding presence, the confidence, the magnetic personality, and charisma—are not accidents of genetics.

Bo came from a lower-middle-class family, where he had a tough father. He graduated from high school but never went on to college. "I have a Ph.D. from the streets," Bo likes to brag. Before becoming a police officer, he worked as a laborer, including a job in construction, where he walked the high steel above Battery Park, helping to build the World Trade Center's twin towers.

Although he had the best record of any NYC policeman at the time, his insistence on getting the job done made him unpopular with his commanding officers. *New York* magazine observed, "Dietl remained an anticrime cop for twelve years—anyone with his record of arrests and convictions would have been promoted to the detective division years sooner."

When Dietl and his partner, Thomas Colleran, caught the two men who raped and tortured a nun in an East Harlem convent, the department brass was embarrassed because the two cops weren't even supposed to be working on the case. Result: Bo's promotion to detective was delayed for six months. "I only got the gold shield because I stormed down to headquarters when I heard my promotion had been rescinded," says Bo. "I slammed my shield down on the desk right outside the police commissioner's office and threatened to quit."

But the same dedication to excellence and results that held Bo back as a civil servant have helped propel him to the top in the business world; he's now a successful entrepreneur who owns a dozen businesses and extensive real estate holdings. With his real estate partner, Steven Witkoff, Bo owns a number of buildings in New York City, including the Woolworth Building in downtown Manhattan and other landmark properties.

Unlike the stereotypical tycoon, Bo is not a self-centered snob who only looks out for himself. Although no longer a cop, he detests bullies and is not afraid to rush to anyone's aid in any physical confrontation or situation involving danger. "Bo is passionately against bullies and for underdogs," says his friend, writer Nicholas Pileggi. "If you're in trouble, boy—you don't want anybody but Bo Dietl around." Writer Ken Gross calls Bo "a complete sentimentalist, willing to back it up with extravagant force."

A highly moral man, Bo, now in his mid-fifties, has dedicated himself to protecting children, particularly from child molesters and neglect. One of his companies makes software that parents can use to monitor their children's Internet activities.

In this book, Bo convincingly makes the case that the principles, attitudes, beliefs, and habits that make him or anyone else successful in business can be learned—and then he shares them with you. Through diligent application of these twenty simple principles, you can take your business success to the next level— and enjoy yourself more, too.

None of these principles is complex or difficult; all are easily within your grasp to master and apply. Of course, you may not like all twenty principles equally, and a few may not fit your personality or situation. No problem! Use whatever works, and don't worry about the rest. Even one of these principles, taken seriously and applied diligently, can help you achieve your goals more quickly and easily than ever before.

A note on the title

Business Lunchatations may strike you as an odd title. You may be thinking, *What the heck does that mean?* But once you get to know Bo—and you will after reading this book—it will make sense to you. Bo has developed a unique personality and style that are his trademarks. They make him stand out, and they make him memorable—two important principles of his business success.

Part of that style is an unusual vocabulary, a unique way of speaking that came naturally to him. As he told me jokingly, "I talk good when I drink." For instance, his real name is Richard Dietl, not Bo Dietl. But today, everybody calls him "Bo," although he uses the more formal "Bean" for business (as in Beau Dietl & Associates). He got the name while in high school. Bo explains, "I had a bad memory for names. I could never remember the names of the other kids. So when I saw them in the hall and they said hi to me and called me by name, I said, 'Hey, Bo!' back to them, hoping they would think I was just being informal and not realizing I didn't know who they were. But everyone caught on to what I was doing, and they soon started calling me Bo in return, and the name just sort of stuck!"

A unique vocabulary of made-up words naturally flows out of

Bo. He spontaneously started calling lunch "lunchatations," and his word for being fussy or picky comes out as "pick-a-tatious."

But Bo is an adult now, not a high-school kid. So why does he still stick with this seemingly silly, made-up language? He does it for a very deliberate reason: "I play stupid to see if the other person is listening to me," he says. Once again, nothing he does is by accident; each action has a purpose that helps propel Bo toward achieving even greater levels of wealth and prosperity.

A short glossary of Bo Dietl's favorite terminology is included at the end of this book, so if you ever happen to meet Bo at Rao's, his favorite restaurant, or if you hire his firm to do an investigation for your corporation, you'll know what he's saying right off the bat.

Robert W. Bly

January 3, 2005

People judge a book by its cover, so make your cover look great.

The first thing you notice when you meet Bo Dietl is his commanding, almost domineering, physical presence.

You think he is a big man until you stand next to him. Then you realize that although he is physically imposing, he is of average height— actually, slightly smaller—just five-foot-eight.

But at just five feet eight inches, Bo tips the scales at slightly more than two hundred pounds . . . and none of it is fat. "Feel my arm," he told me during our first meeting. "Feel my leg." I did, and it was rock-hard: solid muscle.

An article in *GQ* observed: "With a permanently puffed chest and muscled arms that rest a few inches from his body, Dietl has rounded, winning facial features that shine, then burst, with emotion. He wears custom-made suits so sharply tailored you could slice your fingers on the lapels."

The muscle isn't just for show. Bo is the most physically fearless man I know. During his sixteen years as an NYPD police officer, he made more than 1,400 felony arrests, 95 percent of which ended in convictions. At the time, the average cop made 120 arrests during the same career span.

Many of these involved physical confrontations, in which he almost always triumphed—often over taller, heavier opponents. But it was not without a price: While working as a decoy in the anticrime unit, Bo was mugged more than five hundred times, hospitalized more than thirty times, stabbed, shot at, beaten, run over, and pushed down a flight of subway stairs.

■　　　■　　　■

So I wasn't born a "big man," but that's the presence I convey today. And it isn't by accident.

To impress the girls, I began lifting weights while in high school. But just like in my businesses, I don't believe in doing anything the average way. I dedicated myself to fitness with a vengeance, bulking up with a routine of push-ups, sit-ups, and squat thrusts, and was soon performing feats of strength worthy of Charles Atlas. No wonder that actor Stephen Baldwin lifted weights every day for six weeks and bulked up by eating five meals a day to prepare to play me in the movie *One Tough Cop*.

Although you may find this hard to believe, I became strong enough to lift a car by one end and move it. As a policeman, when I found a vehicle parked illegally, I would sometimes amuse the other guys, my fellow officers—and punish the offender—by lifting the car onto the sidewalk.

I soon became the unofficial arm-wrestling champion of the New York Police Department. Challenges came from every precinct, but no other New York City cop could pin my arm to the table—and these are some of the toughest guys in the country. Finally, they brought in a ringer. He was a huge bruiser, and I didn't know he had been the arm-wresting champion in Hungary or some other country in Europe. When we sat down at the table, I was shocked that I couldn't easily pin the guy's arm down. We were deadlocked for about a minute. Then slowly our arms began to descend to the tabletop—in the wrong direction!

It was the first and last time I lost an arm-wrestling match.

I learned another lesson from arm wrestling and weight lifting: Dealing from a position of strength gives you better leverage than dealing from a position of weakness. Most often, just having power is enough to help you win in any situation, without ever having to exercise that power. But sometimes you have to unleash the weapons you have at your disposal—and demonstrate to the other party that you have the upper hand.

For instance: My father, Frank, was a tough guy. He never drank, but he used to rough me up—with a belt—since I was a kid. He was one of those tough, working-class men who tried to keep his kids from becoming bad with the only method he knew: using his hands.

One day when I was seventeen, and long after I began my weight-lifting routine, he raised his hand to strike me. I grabbed his arm and said, "No more, Pops."

Surprised and bewildered, he could not believe that I had the strength to hold his arm in place. I could have easily overpowered him or thrown him to the ground, but after all, he *was* my father.

After we stood immobile like this for a time, I let him go.

That was the last time he ever tried to hit me. When I got older, I'd try to tell him that I understood. I'd tell him that I loved him. And he would pull away. After his stroke, when he couldn't help himself, I'd pick him up in my arms, and I'd kiss him and hug him. He couldn't pull away anymore.

So what does weight lifting and bodybuilding have to do with my success both as a police officer and a businessman? I believe that people instantly judge other people based on the first impression they make—and a large part of that first impression is physical.

Most people think physical appearance is limited to dress and grooming. But it starts one layer deeper: with your body itself. If your body is flabby or weak, or if you lack physical energy, that impression is immediately conveyed to others. My friend, ad man Donny Deutsch, is a great example of the confidence bestowed by physical strength. Donny built himself up at the gym. Now he has big arms and wears a T-shirt to show them off. Knowing he looks big and strong gives him confidence in his business dealings.

Be honest with yourself; have you ever thought of an obese person, *If she can't even discipline herself enough to control her weight, how can I trust her to control my business if I hire her?*

Have you ever been turned off by a salesperson with bad breath or bad teeth? Or who seemed to barely be able to lug his sample case up a flight of steps without huffing and puffing? Or have you ever had an immediate negative impression of a job candidate you were interviewing because his hair was too long or was tinted purple?

You may think that judging people by the way they look or dress is petty and unfair, but petty and unfair or not, we all do it, almost all of the time. We are attracted to, have respect for, and trust people who dress well and keep their appearance presentable. We admire people who are lean, fit, and strong—and are repelled to a degree by those who seem unfit, weak, or sickly.

Fair? Maybe not. But it's human nature, and it's how you will be judged. So why not do everything you can to create a great first impression with the physical you?

"The success of any personal encounter begins the second someone lays eyes on you," says image consultant Lillian Bjorseth, the president of Duoforce Enterprises. "A professional image—appearance and behavior—helps start the experience in the right vein, since people decide ten things about you within ten seconds of seeing you."

A study at the University of California found that when people meet, 55 percent of the impression formed is based on appearance, 38 percent on voice quality, and only 7 percent on what is actually said.

But I go beyond just being clean and neat in my appearance. Through years of constant exercise, I've built myself up, and kept active and in shape.

Now, I'm not saying all this to show off, or because I like the way it looks on paper. I'm saying what I'm saying because it's true. If you want to get ahead, you should look the part. That's why I advise most people to exercise on a regular basis.

I recommend a combination of aerobics (to achieve cardiac fitness and physical stamina) and weight training (to build a muscular body). If you've never been to a gym before and don't know how to exercise properly, you can take a class or sign up for a few sessions with a personal trainer. But don't let a lack of knowledge or laziness hold you back. With the exercise craze in this country in full swing, and gyms popping up in every town, the equipment and knowledge for getting in shape is more accessible than ever.

Anyone can exercise and get in better shape today. If you can't afford a a gym membership, you can do aerobics or lift weights at home; you can buy a basic exercise video for less than the price of dinner for two in a restaurant.

Is lack of time your excuse for not exercising? Well, do you ever watch TV? Then simply turn off the TV and you will have the time to work out. You have to make a choice as to which is more important to you—staying fit or watching *The Apprentice*.

When you have a hard body underneath your business suit, that hardness and fitness help create a more impressive appearance. People can sense that you are a strong person, and will treat you accordingly.

And I take pains to dress impeccably. While working on this book together, Bob Bly showed me an article about me that ran in *The New York Times*, where they mentioned how I have "worked hard" on my "look." I don't know if that's news, fit to print or otherwise, but I can't argue with it.

The importance of dress was impressed on me from early

childhood. I grew up in the Ozone Park section of Queens, where local tough guys always dressed sharp. I was voted "best dressed" when I graduated from Richmond Hill High School in 1968.

I was something of a clotheshorse. I didn't trust my own mother to iron my shirts. You have to spray the fabric with starch, then you iron the back first, so that when you get to the front, it's fresh. This is an image that most of the almost two thousand criminals I arrested would have a difficult time picturing: One of New York's toughest cops fussily ironing his laundry.

My suits cost thousands of dollars each. The cuff links are diamond, sapphire, and gold. I get my cuff links custom-made from Mike, a Russian with his own counter in New York's diamond district. The ties are pure silk; the shoes are the finest Italian leather.

A friend and associate of mine, Mark Arzoomanian, had just hired a new CEO to run one of his companies. I looked at his shoes and saw that they were worn and scuffed. No successful person wears ratty shoes. I told my friend, "Be careful. This guy you hired isn't the big success he claims; he's a scam artist." Sure enough, the CEO ended up running off with a huge amount of money that my friend had loaned to him.

Again, you may find these things superficial, but they are important. Like Bjorseth said, people make instant judgments about people based on a first impression that is formed within ten seconds of meeting someone. Physical appearance is responsible for a large portion of that first impression.

And as Will Rogers is famous for saying, you never get a second chance to make a first impression. So if you show up at a first meeting with spaghetti sauce on your tie and a five o'clock shadow, that's how your customer, client, or new boss will think of you for years to come.

If I had my choice, I would make the latest dress trend in the corporate world—casual Friday—illegal. It is inexcusable to show up for a business meeting wearing leisure clothes. It shows the other person that you don't take the meeting seriously. Imagine a lawyer coming to court without a suit on!

The rule of thumb: Dress at least as well as the customer, and preferably one step higher.

It's so important to dress well every day. When you are dressed nicely, you feel right and can command respect. People look at someone who dresses up differently than they do someone who is dressed poorly, or who is unfit or ungroomed.

Fair or not, when you have a slovenly appearance, people equate that with laziness. They think that if you cannot even take care of yourself, you will not be able to take care of your job. Here are a few of my guidelines for men's appearance in business:

- Wear a three-piece or double-breasted suit, freshly cleaned and pressed.
- Wear a starched cotton shirt, always ironed—white shirts give the best first impression.
- Use cuff links instead of buttons.
- Wear a wedding ring if you are married; one other ring (for example, a class ring) is acceptable—no pinkie rings.
- Wear a fine watch: it's a sign of success.

- Don't wear earrings or other body piercings.
- Wear your hair short and conventionally cut—no long hair.
- Keep your mustache and beard neatly trimmed.
- Clean. Shower daily. Use deodorant and cologne.

And for women:

- Wear a tailored suit.
- Wear blouses with sleeves; keep all buttons on the blouse buttoned except the top one.
- Keep a conservative haircut—no beehives, spikes, or purple, orange, or blue hair.
- Don't overdo your makeup, and go easy on the perfume.
- Wear shoes—not sandals—and stockings are a must.
- Don't wear body piercings, except earrings.
- No bare midriffs, miniskirts, or other revealing outfits.

I also agree with an article I read in *Esquire* (the September 2004 issue), which said that if the sleeve of your jacket covers your shirt cuff, it's too long; about an inch of the shirt cuff should be visible.

As for pants, avoid "flood pants"—pants so short that when you sit, skin shows between the bottom of your pant legs and the top of your socks. In a standing position, pants should ideally reach your shoes without causing more than the slightest break in the crease.

Look in any of my closets (and keep in mind that I own several homes in which I keep full wardrobes), and you will find fifty handmade double-breasted suits, all woven out of fine Australian wool (Super 150 to Super 200); at least three hundred silk neckties; one hundred pairs of Brioni socks; one hundred custom-made Ascot Chang cotton shirts ranging in shades from egg white to robin's-egg blue, and all with French cuffs.

Most days—and nights—you can find me wearing a $5,000 suit with an $1,800 crocodile belt. Under my suit jacket, I carry a blunt-handled, eleven-shot Glock nine-millimeter pistol.

I keep a handkerchief in my left jacket pocket, usually letting some color peek out. I iron my own handkerchiefs—four points, the seams on the inside, the puffy side out—although I could easily have someone else do it for me.

On my left wrist, I wear either a $20,000 Cartier tank watch, or one of a dozen others—Rolex, Bulgari Vacheron Constantin, and Patek Philippe among them. I also wear an 18-karat-gold ring on the ring finger of my right hand.

If you become disheveled during the workday—a rip in your pants, a food stain on your tie, a button missing from your jacket sleeve—fix it immediately. I always remove my jacket when I'm about to eat, and I keep four spare suits in the back of my BMW 645CC—like Batman carrying an extra costume in the Batmobile. And just like Bruce Wayne, where one car in the Batcave wasn't enough, I keep a Bentley GT and a Mercedes 600 SL, among others, in my garage.

Granted, the average man or woman cannot afford to dress like this. But there are also a lot of people who can afford to dress like me and don't. So is my elaborate wardrobe perhaps overkill?

Think about it—people drive a Lexus or other luxury car mainly to give the impression to others who see them that they are successful and wealthy. But you are only in the car while you are driving. And most of your business is conducted inside an office, so often other people don't even see your car.

But you are always in your clothes at work. So, as much as I love the cars, it is the clothes by which others primarily judge you. If you wear a $1,000 suit, the other person assumes that you can afford it, and that says something about you and the level of success you have achieved.

On the other hand, if you are still wearing your confirmation or Bar Mitzvah suit, with wrinkles, holes in the elbows, and a frayed collar, that also says something about you and the level of success you have achieved—something that you probably don't want other people to think.

People will lease their automobiles, because leasing allows them to drive a more expensive car than they could afford to buy outright. So spending beyond one's budget to make a first impression is standard operating procedure in today's society.

Adapt the same procedure to your wardrobe. Even if you are a young executive starting out on a limited salary, own at least one suit that costs more than you could normally afford. As your earnings increase, expand your wardrobe accordingly.

One additional benefit of physical exercise, meticulous dress, and good grooming is not just that you impress others, but that you feel more confident and energetic yourself. I learned this from my sixteen years on the street as a New York City police officer. When someone comes at you with his fists or a knife, you can handle the situation a lot more confidently knowing that you could knock him out with one punch, if you had to. My strength and confidence have often allowed me to make arrests without coming to blows with the suspects.

Similarly, if you want to deal from a position of strength in business, you must project an image of strength. That includes the total package that is you: dress, grooming, health, fitness, weight, posture, body language, mannerisms, and voice. Fair or not, people judge you by the way you look. So, if you want to be perceived as the best in your business, you must always look your best.

2

Success is a full-time job.

In the movie *Wall Street*, a colleague invites Michael Douglas's character, Gordon Gekko, to lunch. Gekko scornfully declines, informing the colleague, "Lunch is for losers." The message: If you want to achieve outrageous success, you have to work at it 24/7; reaching the top in your field is not a nine-to-five job.

While I wouldn't decline a "lunchatation" invitation—because networking at meals is a key part of my business strategy—like Gekko, I believe hard work and single-mindedness of purpose are key factors to achieving success.

Recently, I hired a new president at Beau Dietl & Associates. Practically the first week he was there, we had to prepare a major proposal. He worked all Sunday on it, even going into the office on the weekend rather than doing it at home. I liked that—he showed me he was in the game.

Never allow yourself to stagnate. I have always—first as a detective and today as an executive—desired to be the best; I never bought into the civil-service mentality of mediocrity that so many of my fellow police officers bought into.

During my time with the NYPD, promotions were based not on job performance but on an officer's ability to pass an elaborate series of tests. The tests focused mainly on knowledge of administrative police procedures—for instance, which forms had to be filed when making an arrest for a particular crime—and not on things that actually mattered in doing the job. Basically, if you memorized a couple books, you got promoted up the ladder. Take three tests and you're on top: sergeant, lieutenant, and then captain.

Because the tests were so lengthy and complicated, many of my fellow officers lobbied for easy desk jobs, which gave them more time to study, which in turn helped them pass the tests and get promotions. As a result, the least effective police officers rose in the ranks while effective cops who got results were passed over for promotions. Despite this, I refused to play the game; I spent my time on the streets catching criminals, not at a desk studying to take an exam.

I don't like it when people don't do their jobs. When I was with the NYPD, 90 percent of the police wanted just to get through their day with the least resistance; it was the 10 percent who really believed in their jobs who made the difference.

Once I was in my patrol car when a 1013 came in over the radio. That means "officer needs assistance." I saw two patrolmen sitting in their car, not moving, reading books and studying for the sergeant's test. I drove up behind them and rammed the front of my patrol car into the back of theirs. "Didn't you hear the radio?" I yelled at them. "There's a ten-thirteen in progress and you're sitting here reading a f—ing book. Get your asses going!" Because I am who I am, they knew what I was capable of, and they went.

We had a room in the precinct where we would put up all the officers' names and a list of the arrests each of us made. Mine went on for pages and pages. Finally, some of the old-timers came up to me and said, "Bo, you are embarrassing us." I didn't care. I was there to do my job.

I firmly believe that people are born with either a type A or a type B personality. The A personalities, like me, are the driven achievers: aggressive, bold, energetic, extroverted, and proactive. The B personalities, like many of my fellow police officers who preferred to sit at desks rather than get out into the streets, are typically more conservative, more passive, and introverted. They often like to be part of a hierarchical management structure in which someone else tells them what to do, so they in turn can get the work done by telling others what to do.

However, you are not doomed to mediocrity by your personality type. If you are a B personality, you can transcend your typical behaviors and achieve anything that you want in your business and your career—just by emulating the success principles outlined in this book.

I'm always "on." I'm a hands-on executive—constantly guiding the activities of the investigators and executives who work for me at BDA. Very little of importance goes on at BDA, especially concerning an assignment for a corporate client, that I don't know about, monitor, comment on, or approve of.

I once heard a story told about legendary advertising genius Claude Hopkins.

Claude's boss frequently bragged that Hopkins accomplished twice as much as anyone else at his ad agency. When asked how he could accomplish so much, the agency president replied: "By working twice as hard as anyone else."

I've modified that formula a bit. I try to work three times as hard as the people around me.

In his *New York* magazine profile of me, Nicholas Pileggi wrote: "He made arrests after hours and on his days off. Some of the department's nine-to-five desk officers got crazy processing his paperwork from when he wasn't even supposed to be working."

I like to enjoy myself—whether that means traveling aboard a private first-class jet with the wealthy men I protect, or dining at Manhattan's finest eateries, or playing eighteen holes of golf. But these are never pure social occasions. One of the most important aspects of my business success has been my ability to get results through, with, and for other people, and I believe networking is the most effective tool for this.

Some CEOs make strategic planning their #1 priority. Others place product research and development or operations at the top of their lists. But whatever their priorities, you can be sure that the successful CEOs are thinking about it—and working on it—almost all the time.

As for me, I give the task of building my network of business contacts the same level of dedication, effort, and attention that some other chief executives give to strategy or operations—and it has paid off in spades.

There is a price to pay for business success. For me, it is being out there all the time. I am out doing business networking every night of the week, which has made it impossible for me to be with my family during the week.

There are some executives and entrepreneurs who work only nine to five, but they are a shrinking minority. Most successful executives, myself included (and perhaps you, too) put in hours that would be grueling by the standards of our parents' generation. According to David Berlind in *Tech Update*, thanks to technology (I'm never without my cell phone), we now have "a culture in which the lines between business and home life and work and leisure are blurring."

You may have heard the old saying, "Never mix business with pleasure." My personal philosophy is that there is no dividing line between business and pleasure. I love what I do and the people I surround myself with. We may be having a drink and talking one minute, and then the conversation slides seamlessly into what may become a multimillion-dollar business deal.

I get up naturally at about 7:00 A.M. without an alarm clock, but I like to take my time in the morning. So I read my favorite newspapers at home—the *Daily News,* the *New York Post,* the *Wall Street Journal*—while making business calls from the kitchen table. I drive myself from my home in the suburbs—no chauffeur. I like to be in the office at my desk by 9:30 A.M.

These days, I stay in the office until around 6:30 P.M, and then my "second job" begins: power networking. And I do this every night of the week—virtually no exceptions. When you know people, you can get things done so much more quickly—and I know just about everyone!

When I first started Beau Dietl & Associates in 1985, I would get home from nights of power networking at 2:00 or 3:00 every morning. But today, I prefer to be home and in bed no later than midnight. When you stay out until two or three in the morning, you're no good for work the next morning.

Also, effective business networking does not go on beyond midnight. If you go to the clubs and it is 2:00 or 3:00 in the morning, no one worth knowing is there. The only people out at 3:00 in the morning are the degenerates who don't have jobs and don't have to get up and go to work the next day. I tell my daughter, "Any time you stay out past midnight, you are asking for trouble!"

There is an old Caribbean saying: Some people wait for things to happen; some people make things happen; and some people say, "What happened?" Like most truly successful businesspeople, I'm proactive. I make things happen.

Don't wait for an invitation to make a difference in your company; don't wait for a plum assignment, a nod of approval from a boss, or the opportunity to join your dream team or work on your ideal project (although there's nothing wrong with waiting for a signed contract). Make your own opportunity; start making a difference on the first morning of the first day of your new job or business.

For instance, on my first day of training at the Police Academy, I was on the roof of the building in my training uniform along with the other recruits in my class. Looking down, I saw a man scrambling down the fire escape of a nearby building—but spotted no smoke or fire.

I broke away from the class, ran down to the street, chased the guy for two blocks, and then caught him with two diamond rings that had been stolen from an apartment in the building. My first day of training, and I was already on the street collaring criminals!

I have no tolerance for bureaucrats who stand in the way of those who want to go to work and get results. When I was on the NYPD, I would sometimes bend the law if it meant getting a dangerous criminal off the street. As a consequence, I was often under the scrutiny of Internal Affairs. But it wasn't like I was going to take that sitting down. I told them, if you have something on me, suspend me; otherwise, get out of my way and let me do my job.

There are two schools of thought that conspire to discourage us from hard work. The first is the idea that one should work smarter, not harder. But the truth is that there are already a lot of smart people out there—some of them perhaps even smarter than you.

So, while working smart can give you some kind of edge, working both smarter and harder is a much more formidable weapon against your competitors.

The other school of thought discouraging us from striving at work is the new emphasis on work-life balance, which seems to say that if you work too hard, your personal life will suffer, so don't work so hard, and enjoy your life instead. The fact is, however, that the harder you work, as a rule, the more money you make, all other factors being equal.

America, for example, offers its citizens what is probably the highest standard of living in the world. And that is because we work harder: In 2003, American employees worked an average of 1,792 hours, or 34.5 hours per week (this number seems low because it includes holidays, vacations, and sick days).

In France and Germany, workers average less than 28 hours per week. From 1970 to 2002, the number of hours that the average American works per week increased 20 percent, the most of nineteen countries surveyed by the Organization for Economic Cooperation and Development. By comparison, work hours declined seventeen percent in Japan and twenty-four percent in France.

An article in the *Wall Street Journal* states, "Americans have grown richer than citizens in other industrial nations because they are working more." And Daniel Hacker, an economist with the Bureau of Labor Statistics, says, "Analysis of long-term trends in hours of work has shown that persons working long hours generally have higher earnings."

Peter Kuhn, an economist at the University of California, says that 20 percent of American men work more than fifty hours a week. As a reward, they get larger salaries and bonuses.

Successful people do much more than the work that is merely required by their job description; they go far beyond. Through hard work and long hours, you can build your value to your employer and customers so that you become indispensable. You won't be fired, and your earnings will soar.

Our founding fathers did not work from nine to five, Monday through Friday. For the first 150 years or so of our nation's history, Americans largely worked a six-day week. The forty-hour limit sought by labor unions wasn't imposed until 1940. And if you want to achieve extraordinary success, you won't reduce your efforts because unions tell you to: You'll put in as much effort as it takes to add maximum value to the products and services that your company sells.

I have never settled for just performing the duties my job descriptions required, and my results speak for themselves.

As police detectives in 1981, my partner and I worked during our off-hours and went beyond our beat to develop leads resulting in the capture of two thugs who had raped and tortured an East Harlem nun. Mayor Ed Koch called this case the most heinous crime in New York City history.

When we broke the case, it capsulized one of the most beautiful moments in my life—along with the birth of my kids and meeting Ronald Reagan for fifteen minutes in the Oval Office. If you had a bag with a million dollars in cash and offered me that instead of the feeling I had, I'd have kept that feeling.

Three years later, I helped capture the murderer responsible for the "Palm Sunday Massacre," in which eight children and two adults were found shot to death in their apartment.

Everyone has twenty-four hours in a day, but not everyone uses the time allotted to them to achieve the business and personal results they want. The harder and more effectively you work, the greater your rewards will be.

10 TIME-MANAGEMENT TIPS FOR GREATER PERSONAL PRODUCTIVITY

1. *Master modern technology.* Every professional and middle manager who wants to be more productive should use a modern personal computer with the latest software. Doing so can double, triple, or even quadruple your output.

Install on your computer the same software that your colleagues, other departments within your organization, vendors, and business partners use. The broader the range of your software, the more easily you can open and read files from other sources.

Constantly upgrade your desktop to eliminate too-slow computer processes that waste your time, such as slow downloading of files or Web pages. If you use the Internet a lot, get the fastest access you can. Broadband is getting cheaper by the month and is well worth the money at its current price levels.

2. *Don't be a perfectionist.* "I'm a nonperfectionist," said Isaac Asimov, author of 475 books. "I don't look back in regret or worry at what I have written."

Alfred De Musset wrote, "Perfection does not exist. To understand this is the triumph of human intelligence; to expect to possess it is the most dangerous kind of madness."

Be a careful worker, but don't agonize over your work beyond the point where the extra effort no longer produces a proportionately worthwhile improvement in your final product. Be excellent, but not perfect. Customers do not have the time or budget for perfection; for most projects, getting 95 to 98 percent of the way to perfection is good enough.

3. Don't be pressured to be an innovator. As publisher Cameron Foote observes, "Clients are looking for good, not great." Do the best you can to meet the client's or your boss's requirements. They will be happy. Do not feel pressured to reinvent the wheel or create a masterpiece on every project you undertake.

Don't be held up by the false notion that you must uncover some great truth or present your boss with revolutionary ideas and concepts. Most successful business solutions are just common sense packaged to meet a specific need.

4. Switch between tasks. Even if you consider yourself a specialist, do projects outside your specialty. Inject variety into your project schedule. Arrange your schedule so you switch from one assignment to another at least once or twice each day. Variety, as the saying goes, is indeed the spice of life.

5. Don't work on projects you don't have. Working on assignments that you have not yet received is a waste of time. Be proactive, but don't be foolish. Get letters of agreement, contracts, purchase orders, and budget sign-offs before proceeding.

6. Set a deadline. Productive people set and meet deadlines. Without a deadline, the motivation to do a task is small to nonexistent. Tasks without assigned deadlines automatically go to the bottom of your priority list.

Having a specific date and time for completion eliminates confusion and gives you motivation to get the work done on time. At the same time, don't make your deadlines too tight. Try to build in a few extra days for the unexpected, such as a missing piece of information, a delay from a subcontractor, a last-minute change, or a crisis on another project.

*7. **Protect and value your time.*** Productive people guard their time more heavily than the gold in Fort Knox. They don't waste time. They get right to the point. They may come off as abrupt or dismissive to some people, but they realize they cannot give everyone who contacts them all the time that each person wants. They choose who they spend time on and with. They make decisions. They say what needs to be said, do what needs to be done—and then move on.

*8. **Stay focused.*** As Robert Ringer observed in his best-selling book *Looking Out for Number One,* successful people apply themselves to the task at hand until the work gets done. They concentrate on one or two things at a time. They don't go in a hundred different directions.

*9. **Set a production goal.*** Workers and organizations that want to meet deadlines and succeed set a production goal and stick with it. An individual who truly wants to be productive sets a production goal, meets it, and then keeps going until he or she can do no more for the day.

*10. **Do work that you enjoy.*** When you enjoy your work, it really isn't work. Balance "must-do" mandatory tasks with things that are more fun for you. Seek assignments that are exciting, interesting, and fulfilling.

3

Who you know is more important than what you know.

Do you remember the old commercials that used the phrase, "Bo knows"?

They were right, I do. And what I know is—practically everyone.

When I first met with Bob Bly to discuss writing this book together, he mentioned that he had been an advertising manager for Koch Engineering in New York City, a wholly owned subsidiary of Koch Industries, the conglomerate property of the billionaire Koch brothers of Wichita, Kansas.

"Oh, I know David Koch," I said. I even remembered that David had once run for vice president of the United States as a Libertarian. David's main reason for running was to support the party's presidential candidate, Ed Clark; by becoming Clark's running mate, David was no longer restricted in the amount of money he could donate to the campaign, since he was part of the ticket.

Now, should you or anyone else be impressed because I knew David Koch and could toss out some fast facts about him? No. Did it make a difference with Bob and help push along our business relationship? Perhaps.

I'm a pretty tireless networker. Most people know this about me, but I'm still selective in choosing the people I associate with: My networking inner circle consists almost exclusively of the rich, famous, and powerful—the kind of people who can do things for you if you do things for them (people like famed radio personality Don Imus; super-stock trader Jim Cramer, founder of TheStreet.com; billionaire industrialist David Koch; actors Stephen Baldwin, Denzel Washington, Chris Noth, and Bruce Willis; bestselling author Nicholas Pileggi; screenwriter Nora Ephron; baseball player Mike Piazza; and fashion executive Sheldon Brody). That's just a small sampling of the celebrities, executives, politicians, and entertainers you can find in my personal Rolodex, and if you think I'm mentioning them here just to drop names, you're missing the point entirely.

I am out there networking all the time, every night, socializing and making contacts. Sometimes it means that I get to have dinner with my family only on the weekend, but every night is an opportunity to go out and meet people. New York is such a great city because if you know the right people, you can pick up the phone and make almost anything happen. Donald Trump once told me, "My Rolodex isn't half as big or impressive as yours is!"

"Networking is essential for both new jobs and business contracts," observes Rupert Hart in his book *Effective Networking for Personal Success* (Kogan Page), noting that in a job search, networking is twelve times more effective than answering help-wanted ads.

Every Thursday night, I'm at my regular table at my favorite Harlem restaurant, Rao's. The thing is, I genuinely like the people I socialize with, regardless of the fact that most of them have some degree of influence, wealth, power, or celebrity.

Regulars at my table include singer Paul Anka; Steve Witkoff, my partner in my real estate ventures; Joey "Pots and Pans" DeKama; and entrepreneur Joseph Abboud. Others who have joined me at Rao's for dinner—or who have at least stopped by my table to introduce themselves and say hello—include former GE CEO Jack Welch, Microsoft cofounder Bill Gates, Home Depot founder Ken Langone, famed class-action attorney Mel Weiss, author Victoria Gotti, former NYSE chief Dick Grasso, stock investor Warren Buffett, Jonathan Tisch, and ad man Donny Deutsch. Jack Welch invited only about seventy people to his wedding, and I was one of them.

Warren Buffett told me a story that shows the power of networking. He became friendly with a waiter at a restaurant where he liked to eat. That waiter was Don Keough, who later became CEO of Coca-Cola, a company in which Warren Buffett became a major investor.

Another regular at my table, Hachette Filipacchi ex-CEO David Pecker, introduced me to Dick Wolf, who recruited me to appear as a regular on his TV series *Law & Order*. I also met

JFK Jr. and his wife, Carolyn, with whom I developed a friendship before their tragic demise in an airplane accident.

For me, networking is a critical part of my business and my life. Every night of the week I'm at a top Manhattan restaurant or watering hole, surrounded by executives, entrepreneurs, athletes, politicians, writers, fashion models, clothing designers, and actors.

One night, my friend, top PR executive Marcy Simon, introduced me to Ted Waitt, the founder of Gateway. This led to Ted and me being jointly involved in Syscan, a company that makes LED flat-screen TVs that have higher resolutions than conventional plasma-based flat-screen TVs. All because of a night out on the town.

We usually begin our networking in a back table of the Four Seasons bar. We'll start off with my favorite drink—Ketel One vodka, cranberry juice, soda, and lime—and then smoke some Cuban cigars. I get the best cigars in the world from Al Tomatoes and carry a silver humidor in my car packed with Hoyo de Monterrey Double Coronas, Partagas Lusitanias, and Montecristos. These aren't for me to smoke my lungs out; they're for friends, colleagues, and clients, to make sure everyone who appreciates them is having a good time.

Later, we'll move on to places like Sparks and Elaine's, where on a good night, we're joined by anyone from Gay Talese to Tommy Lasorda or David Wells. Otherwise, we're always with cops, writers, movie stars and producers, celebrities, businessmen, and politicians.

It's important that I always, without fail, pick up the check at the end of the evening—which, given how many people sit at my table, the amount they eat and drink, and the frequency with which I entertain business associates (five nights a week, fifty weeks a year), comes to a considerable expense. This is a part of the cost of doing business.

Always reach for the check first at a business meal, fight for it, and make sure you pay it. If you don't aggressively reach for the check, you will appear cheap and strapped for money. When you pick up the check, the other people get the impression that you are rich and successful; everyone thinks I am richer than I am. And that's important: People want to associate with people who they view as successful, not those who seem to be unsuccessful, cash-strapped, or desperate.

For instance, I recently invited three executives of a large bank in California to a charity golf outing for Big Brothers, an organization I support. They weren't sure the bank wanted to spend the $5,000, which was the donation required for a foursome to play golf, but I wanted to play with them, so I said, "Just come; it's on me."

Now, as comfortable as I may be, $5,000 for a round of golf still isn't peanuts—and I entertain like this all the time. I genuinely wanted to play golf with them, and that's how you start relationships that eventually lead to new business. And, of course, Big Brothers is one of the charities that I endorse.

Other charities I actively support include the National Center for Missing and Exploited Children, The Christopher Reeve Paralysis Foundation, United Cerebral Palsy, New York City Police & Fireman Widow & Children's Fund, CJ Foundation for

SIDS, Tomorrow's Children Fund, Medical Fund of New York, He-mophilia Association, Memorial Sloan-Kettering Cancer Center, Mothers' Voices, and Crohn's and Colitis Foundation of America, to mention only a few.

By telling you this, I'm not trying to convince anyone what a great life I have; I've never denied enjoying myself. The things we do, whether they're obligatory or fun, are all a part of networking. Mainly, though, it's about establishing relationships and getting people to like you.

BOB BLY ON BO

A colleague of Bo's once said, "People want to do business with Bo because they love him."

Bo's dynamic and charismatic personality is enough to instantly captivate most of the people he comes across.

But I don't have that kind of charisma, you might be think-ing. Even so, you can easily replicate the part of Bo's behav-ior that draws people to him:

1. He is open and friendly.

2. He doesn't pretend to be anybody other than himself. You know instantly there are zero pretensions with this man. He is the real thing: himself. And, you can be yourself, too. Nothing is easier.

3. He always tells the truth. You get the sense that he is hiding nothing from you, seeking nothing from you. You feel as if this man would never talk about you behind your back. Do the people you meet feel the same way about you? People feel this way about Bo because they know it's true.

Bo admits loving the high life. As Greg Guss writes about Bo in *Ego* magazine, "He thrives in a room full of people. He lives for the next deal, the next opportunity to further himself and his interests." Bo is not afraid of success, nor is he afraid to make other people his partners and allies in achieving his goals. He cheerfully admits to being a type A personality, and he is well aware that many of us are not.

So, what if you are not a networker? What if you are an introvert? Get over it. You are not ruled by birth, genetics, upbringing, beliefs, or attitudes. You can change yourself and your life to suit your purposes and goals.

You don't have to entirely transform your life into a whirlwind of networking, but you probably should do more than you do now. If you are at home or in your office all the time, you are not meeting people, and it is other people who make our success.

You can't become "just like me" overnight, and maybe you don't want to. But you can become more visible, more outgoing, and more social than you are now.

Here is one easy way: Find and join the local chapter of a trade association or professional society of which your potential customers are members. If there are monthly meetings, force yourself to go at least every other month—even if you don't want to, even if you don't feel like it, even if you are too busy.

An even better approach: Volunteer to be on a committee,

such as one for recruiting new members, finding speakers for meetings, or working on the chapter newsletter. This participation will automatically elevate your visibility and presence to the next level, so the people you hope to do business with start to notice you.

And even better than that: Volunteer to be the speaker at a meeting. Talk about a topic you are comfortable with, one that the audience wants to know more about and that ties in naturally with your product or service. You can't be afraid to get up in front of people and talk. My favorite public-speaking technique is to speak my mind at a press conference, regardless of what would be the politically correct thing to say.

Other people buy your products, hire your company, give you contracts, promote you to new positions, and give you opportunities. The more people you meet, the more people you get to know; and the more people you know, the more likely you are to make a connection with someone who is in a position to help you attain a higher level of success or prosperity in your life.

World-famous marketing expert Jay Abraham noted: "Every one of the relationships you've got is an incredible leverage opportunity. By asking questions, doing more than just going through the process of living life and taking in oxygen and spewing out carbon dioxide, you can achieve amazing things."

Super-salesman Joe Girard explained the mathematics of networking this way: Everyone you meet knows 250 other people. They, in turn, know 250 other people, and so on. Therefore, as you meet new people, your network expands exponentially, not linearly.

For example, there is a photo of me posing with President

George Bush Sr. on the wall at Rao's. The senior Bush appointed me cochairman of the National Crime Commission in 1989. As a result of my volunteer work on that committee, I formed a relationship with the president, which later helped Beau Dietl & Associates get hired to handle security for Bush at the 1992 Republication National Convention.

How do you get started in building your circle of contacts? I have created my own networking environment by making Rao's the focus of my nightly dinners and socializing (although I do network at many other trendy and tony venues).

People know that every Thursday night, they can find me at Rao's. Being the center of attention may not work for you, so the alternative is to network at venues that attract the people who are likely prospects for your business.

There are numerous opportunities to network at venues where people go specifically to do so: networking gatherings, banquets, conferences, trade shows, professional associations, chambers of commerce, and business clubs.

I credit much of my success to being able to transform casual acquaintances into lifelong friendships—and, equally, into career and business opportunities. For example, recently I got a phone call from an associate who was the CEO of a major security technology company. "How would you like me to set up a meeting between you and the Chief Information Officer of General Electric?" I asked my friend after exchanging greetings.

"I'd be thrilled," the technology entrepreneur told me.

"Let me call you back in a few minutes," I said.

After hanging up, I dialed GE and was immediately put

through to CIO Gary Reiner, the number-three man in the organization. How many people do you know who could call GE and immediately get the CIO on the phone? That's the power of networking. A regular salesman could call twenty times and not get to this level, and I did it in fifteen seconds.

As I talked with Reiner, it was obvious that he was not eager to take the meeting; he didn't see the immediate benefit. Some people would have given up, let it go. But not me. I was relentless in pushing for the meeting—and I pushed hard, to the point where others may have feared that Reiner would take offense or get annoyed. But none of that bothers me.

"This guy [the security company CEO] has an important new technology for security, and you're a billion-dollar company," I told Reiner. "Let's get together and see what the opportunity is; maybe it will be something, maybe it will be nothing. But I really want to see you anyway, so this is a great excuse for me to come up to Connecticut."

Sure enough, within a few minutes, I had set up a meeting between myself, the security technology CEO, and GE CIO Reiner. Most important, I made sure everyone agreed on the details. Don't just make a vague agreement to meet with someone. By the time I was done, I made sure everyone had a specific date and time penciled in on their calendars.

The potential benefits? With GE as a partner, the small company might bring to the market an important new technology with applications in defense and homeland security—resulting in huge revenues and profits.

For me, I benefit simply from the company of other people. I wasn't bullshitting when I told Gary I missed him and really wanted to see him. I did!

When you treat networking as a mandatory task rather than as a distasteful chore to be avoided at any cost, you build an incredible, extensive network. It takes time and effort and a lot of work, and it doesn't happen overnight. But when you have it, you can make things happen in minutes—thanks to your contacts and relationships—that would take others months to accomplish, if they happened at all. And that's the power of networking.

And even the most unlikely members of your network can yield unexpected positive results. As a kid growing up in one of Queens's toughest neighborhoods, I became friendly with alleged mobsters John Gotti and Colombo crime family underboss Joey Scopo. The neighborhood was full of wise guys, and because these friends were loyal to me, I remained loyal to them. Later, when we all became adults—me, a member of the NYPD, Gotti and Scopo as alleged members of the mob—my connections prodded me to get involved in solving one of New York's most notorious crimes: the 1981 rape and mutilation of an East Harlem nun.

Fat Tony Salerno said to me, "Bo, what are you doing about the rape of that nun up in Harlem?" and that's when I asked to be assigned to the case.

When I first joined the NYPD, word went out from them to the organized crime families: No one interferes with Bo Dietl; no one involves him in our business; no one asks him for so much as a license-plate check. He is a friend of ours, but he has gone a different way. We respect and like him, and if anyone messes with Bo, we will break his head.

Once, I had a client who was being threatened by organized crime; three goons had been sent to his office and threatened to beat him up unless he cooperated with them.

I sat down with a few of the higher-ups and said, "You live in your world, and I don't interfere with it; but this guy is with me and is under my protection. He is off-limits, and don't mess with him anymore." That terminated the problem for my client.

Another time, Jordan Belfort hired us to do security for his brokerage firm. Organized crime wanted a piece of his operation. They had sent some tough guys to Jordan's offices to shake him down for a cut.

When they showed up with ten goons, I had ten of my own goons—all former cops—to meet them. We were bigger, and we outgunned them. And no criminal in his right mind wants to fuck with a retired cop; you will have the world come down on you if you do.

I told them, "I am now involved. Jordan and his people are now under my protection. This extortion thing is no more. It is over with, ended." And that was the end of that.

I can sit down with these wise guys and buy them drinks and dinner, because they never under any circumstance do their business in front of me. They are always nice to me, and I am not involved in any of their activities.

Once, after doing security work for the first President George Bush, I was offered a high-level position in his administration. Washington, D.C., Judge Reggie Walton, who was checking on my background, was concerned about my alleged "ties to organized crime."

Jim Fox, the assistant director of the New York City office of the FBI, wrote an immediate letter to Judge Walton and to President Bush. He said, "I put my thirty-year career and reputation with the FBI on the line when I tell you that Bo Dietl has no ties or involvement with organized crime, in any sense. Yes, he did grow up with them, and knows many of them, but he has no involvement in any criminal activities of any kind." But I didn't like being questioned in that manner, so I thanked President Bush for his consideration and passed on the appointment.

One of my great advantages is that I am trusted in many circles, not just the police, not just business, not just entertainment, not just politics. That means I can instantly get things done on a high level—things someone without my contacts would find impossible to accomplish.

14 NETWORKING TIPS

Most of us aren't natural networkers like Bo Dietl. Here are fourteen tips that even the most introverted businessperson can use to make valuable friendships and connections.

1. Find low-key learning environments. Business-card exchanges and other networking events are high-pressure situations where people go to meet others but usually do so with all their defenses intact. For more relaxed networking, find educational atmospheres, such as workshops and seminars, where the focus is on learning and where people's defenses are lowered.

2. *Start conversations.* Go out of your way to get into conversations with anyone and everyone you can, in person, on the phone, or via e-mail. Cross the street, cross the room, cross the train to talk to someone. Find out what they're working on and tell them what you're working on. Anything can come out of a simple conversation: ideas, alliances, connections, referrals, new business, new opportunities.

3. *Master the art of small talk.* Find something in common with the other person so you can share information and resources. If they mention something you know nothing about, ask them to explain or elaborate on it. Ask what their challenges are, personal or professional. Then offer an idea, a contact, or some other resource that might help them, laying the groundwork for your follow-up.

4. *Make contact, not contacts.* The goal of networking is not to meet as many people in as short a time as possible. The goal is to find a business community that satisfies your needs, one that brings together people who are your prospects and with whom you are comfortable. So if you attend an event, don't think you have to get to everyone in the room. Meet as many people as you can, but also, if a conversation is going well, stay with it.

5. *Be a good listener.* Don't be worried about what you're going to say. You don't need to perform your sales pitch, just have your blurbs ready to use as a tool to engage people in conversation. Do more listening than talking, and ask a lot of questions. Then simply respond to what you hear. Answer questions, devise solutions, be creative. Sound easy? Just try it.

6. Arrive early. If you wait until most of the attendees are already there, many of them will already be in conversations, and it won't be as easy to break in.

7. Never sit with someone you know. Attend an event with a friend, but put on your name tags and then separate at the door. Otherwise, you will never meet anyone new.

8. Look for wallflowers. Instead of trying to break into conversations that are already going, find someone sitting or standing alone and simply introduce yourself. Do it even if they don't look as though they want to be approached. The apparent standoffishness may merely be a cover for their own discomfort.

9. Use the food to begin conversations. Stand by the buffet and make recommendations to anyone who approaches about what's good (or bad).

10. Keep going back to the buffet. Never put more than three bites on your plate. Take your plate to a crowded table, introduce yourself, talk (and listen) for ten to fifteen minutes, exchange cards, then excuse yourself to get up and get more food. (After all, your plate will be empty.) Repeat this until the room is empty. And don't forget that you can also talk to people while you're in line at the buffet.

11. Be random about where you sit. Although most people do it, you can't tell by how someone looks what will come out of a conversation with them. Don't judge.

12. Make notes about the people you meet. Every time

someone gives you a card, make a point of writing a note on the back—while you're still talking. This will not only flatter, you will also have a much better chance of remembering what you talked about so that you can follow up in a more personal way.

13. Wear a jacket with pockets. Keep your business cards and a pen in your left pocket, and put any cards that you get into your right pocket. That way, you won't be fumbling with cards or accidentally hand a new contact someone else's card.

14. Wear an unusual accessory. If you wear a colorful scarf or tie, you can refer to it when you follow up: "I was the one with the orange scarf."

Source: Ilise Benun, www.artofselfpromotion.com. Reprinted with permission.

4

Use the power of perseverance.

Winston Churchill was once asked to give a commemorative talk to the graduating class of a prestigious university. After he was introduced, he walked up to the podium, stood there, and stared out into the crowd with a grim look on his face. A hushed silence fell over the audience.

Churchill opened his mouth and said four words: "Never, never give up." Then he sat back down, to thunderous applause.

Almost all successful people, myself included, agree on this one success principle: All else being equal, perseverance—the strength, spirit, and guts to go on in the face of overwhelming odds—separates the winners from the losers. Calvin Coolidge perhaps said it best:

Press on. Nothing in the world can take the place of persistence. Talent will not: nothing is more common than unsuccessful men with talent. Genius will not; unrewarded genius is almost a proverb. Education will not; the world is full of educated derelicts. Persistence and determination alone are omnipotent.

"When we see ourselves in a situation which must be endured and gone through, it is best to make up our minds to meet it, meet it with firmness, and accommodate everything to it in the best way practical," said Thomas Jefferson. "This lessens the evil, while fretting and fuming only serves to increase your own torments."

■   ■   ■

During my days in the NYPD, I worked a lot of decoy duty. I would go undercover, dressed as a bum, a homeless man, or a wino, and wait for criminals to rob or mug me. When they tried, they'd be in for a surprise when they discovered that I was not a helpless hobo but an armed, healthy man who would disarm and arrest them.

If the suspect attempted an escape, I never had any trouble running him down. Except one time the mugger was faster than me, so I called for backup. Me and eight other officers ran after the guy, but we still could not catch him.

He went over the tops of cars, knocking people over, and he left us in the dust. Finally, we caught a break: The mugger bumped into someone, which slowed him down for only a second, but it was enough for me and the other cops to catch him and arrest him. It turns out that the reason he was so fast was that he was a professional soccer player from Argentina.

You could say it was pure luck that let me get my man that day—the accident of one person stumbling into another. But I see it differently. We were persistent. We kept chasing him and didn't stop until we caught him.

The reason why perseverance is a key to success is that things change, life isn't stable, and even the most successful people have ups and downs. No one stays at the top all the time.

Stephen Jobs, for example, first brought his idea for a personal computer to wealthy entrepreneur Nolan Bushnell, founder of Atari. Bushnell liked to invest his money in other ventures, but he dismissed Jobs and his idea. Instead of giving up, Jobs pressed forward on his own and cofounded Apple Computer with Stephen Wozniak.

The most successful people in the world are those who persist and refuse to give up. After selling Learjet for many millions of dollars, Bill Lear, toward the end of his life, opened a research laboratory to develop better aircraft engines. He kept working on it, even when he was dying of leukemia. His last words to one of his colleagues were: "Finish it? You bet we'll finish it!"

Of course, not everything you try will be successful. I've lost my share, too. In 1986, I was nominated for the United States Congress by the Republican and Conservative parties of New York State for the 6th Congressional District to fill the seat of the late Joseph Addabbo. In a district where Democrats outnumber Republicans by seven to one, I lost the election to the Reverend Floyd Flake. But amazingly, I lost by only 2,500 votes—one of the closest congressional races in New York history.

Most successful people you talk to had to overcome some kind of difficult challenge, problem, or adversity to get where they are today. One such person is Milo Jones, who ran a small farm in Wisconsin, suffered a paralyzing stroke, and faced financial ruin. But then an idea struck him. He told his relatives to plant the entire field with corn, which they would not sell as a crop but use to feed a herd of pigs. The pigs were then butchered and made into sausage. Today, Jones Dairy Farm Sausage is a major consumer brand, and it made Milo a millionaire many times over.

Those who persevere are successful in the long run, because even when the going gets tough for them, they persist and survive to come back another day. It's important to remain loyal to friends, acquaintances, and colleagues both when they're at the top of their game and when they're down. Stay friendly with influential and powerful people even when they slide down, because if you snub them at the bottom, they'll remember it when they're back at the top.

Similarly, when other people achieve an extraordinary level of success, be genuinely happy for them, and let them know it; petty jealousy is an unhealthy emotion and has no place in business.

For instance, one of my major competitors recently doubled the size of his security firm through a $1.9 billion acquisition. His firm was already larger than BDA, and through the acquisition, his new company pulled even further ahead in size and revenue.

My reaction? I called him and congratulated him. I told him that he had raised the bar for all of us in the industry. He told me, "Of all of the CEOs of the large security firms, you were the only one to call me up and congratulate me. I think everyone else is jealous, except you, Bo."

If you're civil to the competition, then staying loyal to the people who count, friends and business associates, should come naturally—especially in their darkest hours when they need it most. When Dick Grasso stepped down as Chairman of the NYSE and was criticized for the salary he had been paid, I stood by his side.

When CEOs and other high-level executives lose their jobs, their friends often disavow them and leave them. Those fair-weather friends are dickheads. And when those CEOs have recovered and are on their way back up, don't think they won't forget how you treated them.

■   ■   ■

One of the reasons people frequently say they have given up or are not trying very hard is that they are "depressed." I have a solution for that, too.

Refuse to be depressed if everything is not right. Things are rarely perfect for anyone—even for those people who you think have a great life. The key to overcoming depression is action. Don't sit around and worry; don't mope. Do something. Even if it's getting up at 7:00 in the morning and ironing your own shirts, take action.

The worst thing you can do if you lose your business or get fired is sit around the house and let it get you down. If you can't find a job right away, get a paper route and start delivering newspapers; that at least will make you some money and get you up early in the morning. I've been working since age seven, when I had my first paper route and had to get up at 5:30 in the morning to deliver the *Long Island Press* before going to school.

Kids—especially today—are spoiled. They have too much, and they have it too easy; this includes my own kids. Nothing makes you feel better about yourself than getting out there, getting up and around, working, and accomplishing something—anything, as long as it's something.

I am absolutely relentless when it comes to getting the job done. I never quit, and I never give up.

There was a guy in Brooklyn who had killed five people, and I vowed I would track him down and bring him to justice. He knew I was on his trail and tried to frighten me by having me followed, which, of course, didn't scare me in the least.

I went to his girlfriend's house, got the phone number of the house, and called from across the street. I told her, "I want to talk to him [her boyfriend, the murder suspect]." Then I heard him in the background, asking who was on the phone, and I knew he was there. The problem was that I didn't have a warrant to enter the house.

So I called Emergency Services—in New York, we don't have a SWAT team, so you call Emergency Services—and told them I had seen him through a window. Did I actually see him? Maybe I did, maybe I didn't, but the five people he murdered all saw him before it was over. He wasn't playing by Marquis of Queensbury rules, so neither was I.

We broke into the house and . . . he wasn't there. Did I make a mistake? Then I heard noise coming from the ceiling. I climbed up to the top floor, where I found him hiding in a closet, holding a Mac-10 machine gun. I had a shotgun and was going to kill him. But he surrendered, and we arrested him. I was happy with that.

5

Why pay to advertise your business when the media will do it for you for free?

The Imus Show is one of the longest-running and most popular radio programs of all time. Don Imus has been on the radio since 1968.

To run just a single thirty- or sixty-second radio commercial on *The Imus Show*—which has twelve million listeners a day— can cost you anywhere from $1,800 to $2,500; rates vary based on the time of broadcast.

Let's say the average cost to advertise on Imus is $2,000 per minute. If you were to buy a one-hour commercial for your business—assuming they would let you, which they won't—that would cost $120,000. If you ran that commercial every week, within one year you would have spent more than $6 million in advertising.

Well, every Monday, I take a seat next to Imus on his program, for a one-hour segment from 7 A.M. to 8 A.M. or 8 A.M. to 9 A.M. (If you want to tune in, Imus is on WFAN in New York, 660 on the AM dial; the program is also syndicated to radio stations nationwide.) But my company doesn't pay a dime for this exposure. In fact, it's free because I appear as a regular weekly guest. We got to know each other years ago, when Don Imus hired me for security purposes in response to a series of threatening letters he received.

In addition to my regular gig on Imus, I am also a frequent guest on TV, including on FOX News Channel, MSNBC, CNBC, CNN, and all the local New York City TV stations. Feature articles about me have appeared in major publications, such as *The New York Times*, *Crain's New York Business*, *Time Out New York*, *The Wall Street Journal*, *EGO* magazine, *Esquire*, *GQ*, *Cigar Aficionado*, and *New York* magazine.

Unlike Donald Trump, whose father was a well-heeled real estate entrepreneur, I came from a humble lower-middle-class background. So the thought of spending $6 million a year on radio ads is unfathomable to me—even though I can (almost) afford it.

My approach to marketing is a lot more cost-effective than advertising, and it gives me a considerably better return on investment (ROI). The secret: Don't pay for ads when you can get the same—or better—exposure with free publicity.

I don't believe in hiring a publicist to do my publicity for me, and my security company, Beau Dietl & Associates, employs neither a public relations firm nor an advertising agency (although I use Donny Deutsch's ad agency for one of my consumer products companies).

Anyone with common sensation (common sense) can get promotatated (self-promotion). You just have to be yourself.

Rule one of dealing with the press: Be available whenever they call you, at any time of the day or night.

I was working on this book with Bob in my office, while juggling a dozen details of running my businesses at once. Then Maria, my executive assistant, buzzed me. When could I speak with a reporter doing a story on security at the Republican National Convention? My response: "Anytime he wants."

I don't seek free publicity because it feeds my ego (although I don't mind that aspect of it). I do it because it's good for businesses. Bob says I'm a master at building the "Bo Dietl Brand" and "creating buzz." I still think of myself as a New York cop, so talk like that is a little too trendy for me, but if that's what it is, so be it.

What's the logic behind it? According to Bob, it's simple: "In today's world, consumers are tired of dealing with faceless corporations. And they are bombarded by advertising messages and constant communications in all forms. Especially in a service business, like security, it's too easy for potential customers to see all firms competing for their business as being pretty much alike—although in reality, that's not the case at all. The brand that sells Beau Dietl & Associates—and has made it one of the largest and most successful private security firms in the world—is the brand that is Bo."

Byron Kalies, a management consultant and writer, wrote, "Great leaders have stories, legends, myths about them," in

Across the Board, the magazine published by the Conference Board. "If you're a CEO, you need to be noticed."

For me, getting noticed wasn't something I deliberately pursued. It came naturally. People are attracted to a unique personality with style, even in a "serious" business like security. Look at the Slomin's Shield and McGruff the Crime Dog. Everything is branding today.

So through media appearances, I've become a genuine character, and branding that revolves around a character—real or fictional—has a long track record of success. Look at Sam for Breakstone, Mr. Whipple for Charmin toilet paper, Mr. Clean for cleaning fluid, and Tony the Tiger for breakfast cereal.

According to an article in the *Daily News* (9/20/04), the Mc-Gruff ad campaign has resulted in more than twenty million Americans joining neighborhood watches. And the famous Crash Test Dummies campaign for the U.S. Department of Transportation increased seat belt usage from 21 percent to 79 percent of drivers. Then there's Smokey Bear, who reduced the land destroyed in forest fires annually by more than 75 percent.

My big PR break came when Nicholas Pileggi wrote a profile on me, "The Cop Who Came in from the Heat: How the City Lost a Top Detective," for the August 26, 1985, issue of *New York* magazine. After the article was published, I was thrust into the spotlight—and I liked it a lot. I coauthored a book about my career with the NYPD, *One Tough Cop*, which was then made into a movie. I was executive producer of the film.

I like the high profile that the motion picture industry gives me, and sure, I've been bitten by the acting bug, too. I've had small roles in several movies, including *Dead Man's Curve, Carlito's Way, Bad Lieutenant, Whispers in the Dark, Maniac Cop 2, This Is My Life,* and *Goodfellas*. I have also appeared in the TV series *Law and Order* and in the made-for-TV movie *Casualties of Love: The Long Island Lolita Story*. For me, though, it's not really acting: The only roles I take are those of detectives and tough guys—that is to say, I always play some version of myself.

But you're probably not a tough ex-cop, a silver-screen star, or a flamboyant man-about-town. And most likely, *New York* magazine isn't going to do a feature article on you. Does this mean you can't use the same successful PR and personal branding strategies that I've used? Not at all. Everyone is unique in some way. By keying your brand off that unique personality, you can gain visibility, establish awareness of your brand, and stand out from the crowd in your marketplace.

Examples of products sold with a "personal brand" include Carvel Ice Cream (Tom Carvel), Wendy's (Dave Thomas), the George Foreman Grill (George Foreman), Perdue Chicken (Frank and Jim Perdue), Chrysler (Lee Iacocca), and Orville Redenbacher popcorn (Orville Redenbacher).

With the exception of George Foreman, none of these men has a physically imposing presence or was a celebrity prior to becoming the spokesperson for their brand. Yet they have all succeeded beyond their wildest expectations.

Even if you aren't building yourself as your company's brand, there are ample opportunities to take advantage of the power of PR to increase your visibility, status, and sales in your market.

And unlike advertising, where a single commercial during the Super Bowl can cost upwards of a million dollars, an effective PR campaign can be conducted for not much more money than you have in your wallet right now.

For instance, when Eric Yaverbaum, cofounder of the New York City PR firm Jericho Communications and coauthor (with Bob Bly) of *Public Relations for Dummies*, went into PR, his first assignment was to do publicity for an off-Broadway play. The day after it opened, drama critic Frank Rich panned the production in *The New York Times*.

Most publicists would have given up, but not Eric. He immediately issued a press release to all New York media with the headline: "Even *The New York Times* Makes Mistakes."

In it, he stated that *The New York Times* did indeed make mistakes, as in its negative review of the play, and he offered to reward readers who helped him prove it. If you brought in an article from *The Times* with a typo in it to the box office, you would get a free ticket to the play. The ploy gained a lot of publicity for the play, as well as filling the box office (most of those who came for the free ticket had to buy tickets for their companions).

When you have been the feature subject of a movie, and you call a press conference, the media will come. Most businesspeople don't have this advantage. But with a little ingenuity and effort, your PR efforts can overcome that handicap, too.

When Eric handled publicity for Domino's Pizza, he noticed

that whenever there was a national crisis, pizza deliveries to the White House increased, as staffers ordered pies to eat as they worked through the night.

Eric sent out a press release on the "Pizza Meter," in which he announced that the state of national affairs could be tracked, with a high degree of accuracy, by measuring delivery of Domino's pizzas to the White House.

The ploy garnered major media coverage for Domino's— and think about how non-newsworthy pizza usually is. Johnny Carson even talked about the Pizza Meter on *The Tonight Show*.

I get publicity because of the fame I've already developed, as well as because of my personality being what it is, but if that can't work for you, creativity can. When Eric's PR agency was brainstorming for a new publicity angle for Domino's Pizza, his partner said, "It's April. Tax time. On April fifteenth, thousands of New Yorkers are going to be standing on line at the post office, trying to file their tax returns in the last minute before the deadline."

The PR firm told Domino's to deliver dozens of pizzas to the post office around dinnertime on April 15, and to offer it free to anyone there. The stunt garnered major coverage on all New York stations on the evening news. "What was brilliant about this, and it was my partner's idea, not mine," Eric said, "was that calling a press conference is difficult, because you have to convince reporters to come. Instead, with this promotion, we went to where the cameras already were!"

Another way to attract the media is to hire employees who are experts in their fields, because the media is constantly looking to interview experts. If the industry expert works for your firm, the attention they will get from the media will naturally benefit your company, too.

My ex-CEO at Beau Dietl & Associates was the former First Deputy Police Commissioner of New York City, so whenever there was a news story related to security—whether a political convention in town or 9/11—the press would want to interview him. And since he was the CEO of BDA, we directly benefited in publicity from his status as a security expert.

How this can work for you: Send letters to the major media in your industry. Explain that you—or your CEO or whoever is the guru in your company—are indeed an expert on topic X, and let the media know that whenever they are doing a story on topic X, you'll be available for an interview.

You might not think this would work, but it does—all the time. Reporters have to produce a lot of copy under tight deadlines. If you can fill in the missing information they need for their story, they'll happily credit you as the expert source and, in return, generate valuable publicity for your business.

20 RULES FOR SUCCESSFUL SELF-PROMOTION

1. Never tell anyone (unless you have an established relationship with them) that you are not busy and that you are looking for work. Clients want to hire those who are successful, not those who are hungry.

2. Always put your name, address, and phone numbers

on every piece of promotion you produce. This makes it easy for potential new business to reach you.

3. Write a book. It positions you as an expert.

4. If you don't have the time to write a book, write an article.

5. When you write that article, try to get it published in more than one publication. You can change the title and a few of the examples to tailor it to each publication's readers.

6. Regularly mail reprints of your articles to your prospects and clients. Attach a note or short cover letter to personalize the mailings.

7. Advertise your services in magazines aimed at advertising professionals. Try a variety of journals and different ads until you discover which ads give the best results. Also, try both classified and display formats.

8. Use direct mail to generate new business leads. A successful mailing of only a hundred letters can often yield five to ten highly qualified new prospects.

9. Create a package of literature describing your services, background, fees, methods, clients, and so forth. Mail the package to people who request more information in response to your ads and mailings. Such a package is extremely useful in prescreening leads.

10. Publish a free print or online newsletter. Newsletters help build recognition and establish credibility with a select audience (that is, the people who receive the newsletter) over an extended period of time.

11. Don't skimp on letterhead, envelopes, and business cards. Your letterhead design and paper quality can convey an image of class and success.

12. Offer to speak and give seminars before trade associations and professional groups. Make sure potential clients will be among those in attendance.

13. Teach a course at a local college or university—day school or adult education. This establishes you as an "instant expert" in your field.

14. Network. Don't be a recluse. Be social. Attend meetings, seminars, and luncheons. Volunteer to work on a committee. Become visible in the business community.

15. Recycle your content for other promotions. A lecture can become the basis for an article or a series of articles. The articles can be turned into a book. Using your basic content over and over makes it possible to get broad exposure and still have time to devote to your business.

16. Be selective. Not every opportunity to speak, lecture, write, or participate is worthwhile. Focus on those promotional activities, which will give you the most return on your time and effort.

17. Keep your name in front of clients and prospects with a "premium" (free gift). Most will appreciate your thoughtfulness. And the right premium—one that can be kept in the office for years—can serve as a daily reminder of you and your service.

18. Let people know about your recent successes. If your latest assignment was a rousing success, send out a press release to the media and potential clients. When sending your press release to prospects, include a cover note that says, "Here's what I've done recently; let me do the same for *you!*"

19. *Save any letters of praise that you receive from clients, and build a "kudos" file.* Selected quotations from these letters—or even reprints of the letters themselves—can dramatically add to the selling power of your promotion. Be sure to get permission first before you quote someone in print.

20. *Keep written records of past promotions and their results.* Only by measuring the success or failure of promotional experiments can you learn which promotions work for you and which will bomb.

6

If you can't deliver what you promise, you won't be in business for long.

There's an expression in Texas for men and women who can talk the talk but can't walk the walk: "Big hat, no cattle." Some say that if Bo Dietl lived in Texas, he'd have a ten-gallon hat, but he'd also own the largest ranch in the neighborhood.

Bo is more than flash; there is solid substance behind the glitz. Some businesspeople are good at getting publicity; others are good at getting results for their clients. Bo is good at both.

Eric Yaverbaum coined the term "go-to guy" for the expert the media calls when it wants to do a story in a particular field. For management, the go-to guy is Tom Peters; for law, it's Alan Dershowitz; for sex, it's Dr. Ruth; for relationships, it's Dr. Phil; and for security, it's Bo Dietl.

But Bo is more than just talk. Both as a police officer and as head of his own international security firm, Bo gets results—time and time again.

In a case for a major brokerage house, Beau Dietl & Associates uncovered a fraud ring operating out of the company's wire-transfer department, where a brokerage employee was working under the direction of a major organized-crime family in New York. The brokerage employ had arranged on behalf of the crime family a $25 million wire transfer, off the books, to a major bank in Europe. Bo's operatives collected hard evidence and notified the FBI.

Another client, Banker's Trust, hired Beau Dietl & Associates to protect the bank in a lawsuit; clients were suing Banker's Trust to recover $1 billion that they claimed was lost in bad derivatives trades. Bo's investigators discovered that more than thirty other banks were involved in the sale of the securities; the clients were well aware of the risks and had incurred more than $1 trillion in total losses with these banks. "We deflected much of the liability from Banker's Trust," notes Bo.

"You can talk all you want, but unless you get the job done, at the end of the day, that's all it is—talk," says Bo.

Bo's ability to get the job done as a member of the NYPD made him a national celebrity and, once he transitioned to the private sector, a multimillionaire. His advice for businesspeople: Publicity is nice, and media attention can raise your profile, but if you can't deliver the goods, your fame will be short-lived and your success almost nil.

And this is where power networking gives Bo the edge.

■   ■   ■

When you know people, you can quickly and easily get things done that others without your connections would have to work hard at, with only a slim chance of getting the result.

After 9/11, many corporations in New York City became concerned about another terrorist attack. Security became heightened. It was a boom time for the security business.

Estée Lauder had its offices in the General Motors building, then owned by Donald Trump. The head of operations for Lauder was Ed Straw, who had been a three-star admiral in the Marines. He is six-foot-three, built like a tank, a serious, no-nonsense guy—no one messes with him.

I was invited to attend a meeting with Straw and his team in Lauder's boardroom; also in attendance were other security firms competing with Beau Dietl & Associates for the immediate assignment at hand: improving security in the GM building.

They were worried about all sorts of threats. Bombs in the underground parking garage and shoulder rockets were high on the list. Then Admiral Straw asked, "Is Trump worried? What measures is he taking to secure the building?"

Everyone looked at each other, shrugging their shoulders. I whipped out my cell phone, punched in Donald's number, got him on the phone, and said, "Hi, Donald; it's me, Bo." Everyone at the meeting couldn't believe that I could get Donald Trump on the phone that quickly and easily—but when you are a power networker and know everybody, like I do, you can; you don't have to work at it, as your competitors do.

I explained Admiral Straw's concern with GM building security, and then handed my cell phone to Straw. Donald Trump told the Admiral: "You can trust Bo Dietl; he knows what he's doing. Do whatever Bo recommends for building security, and I'll pay half." With one phone call, I had cut the client's security bill in half, arranged to get them the security they wanted, and won a new assignment for BDA.

7

The "catalyst strategy": You don't have to invent a new widget to get rich— you just have to own a piece of it.

With a single phone call in chapter 3, I reached General Electric CIO Gary Reiner and got him to take a meeting with me and a technology company CEO who was developing a new security product. When I told Bob the story, he asked me how I benefited, and I made mention of the company of other people being a reward within itself. As true as that is, there is another layer to be considered.

Yes, it could very easily wind up that I get nothing out of it, if it turns out that GE has no interest in the new product, and if no deal is made.

I don't do these things thinking I'm going to immediately get something in return. But arranging this meeting with GE gives me a stronger relationship with the other CEO, opening up possibilities for the future.

Bob referred to this as a "catalyst strategy," and what it does is allow me to generate revenues beyond the companies and products that I actually own and produce. It works because of the tremendous network of contacts that I work nearly full-time to build, as explained in chapter 3.

It's only natural that people within my network—in business, law enforcement, politics, technology, education, and public service—have mutual interests, complementary technologies, and related projects.

My role as a business catalyst is to (a) keep an eye out for those shared and complementary interests, and (b) facilitate the introductions that begin the relationships between the multiple parties.

Many of these introductions never progress beyond a first meeting, usually because either there is no chemistry or one of the parties isn't interested in pursuing the possibility of a joint venture further, or because the deal isn't right for one of a dozen other reasons. But in other cases, the mutual interests of the two parties can lead to lucrative business ventures. And when they do, even though they're not obligated to reward me financially, more often than not they do the right thing.

The amount of compensation is not negotiated beforehand; in fact, I have no contract or agreement of any kind assuring myself of a finder's fee or any other kind of remuneration.

I get nothing up front. It's all about showing people what I can do for them. I never set my finder's fee in advance, because I feel that the relationships I've forged have a level of trust that eliminates the necessity of contracts. There's no contract, no written agreement, but if something happens, I expect people to remember me as the guy who brought them together.

When the deal is right, I can take a more involved role. For instance, I'm a partner in NetWolves Corporation, the software developer that wrote the code for Bo Dietl's One Tough Computer Cop, a program that helps parents monitor their kids' Internet usage.

The software has been approved by the National Center for Missing and Exploited Children, a nonprofit that I have actively supported through fund-raising, endorsements, and charitable donations. One Tough Computer Cop has also been featured on the TV program *America's Most Wanted*.

Through my GE connections—remember, I was a guest at ex–GE CEO Jack Welch's wedding, and I am on a first-name basis with Gary Reiner, the current GE CIO—NetWolves recently signed an agreement with GE for worldwide installation of Net-Wolves "FoxBox" technology. FoxBox is an intrusion-detection system designed to work with the firewalls of midsize companies.

You could argue that I'm lucky. One of the technology companies I associate with, Soft Works, was launched before the dot-com boom, and at the top, before the bubble burst, my partners and I sold the company for $180 million. I took out millions of dollars in cash as profit and invested the rest into more business ventures.

But most people aren't this "lucky," because they never take action. I was able to cash in on the technology boom because I'm investing in and launching new technology businesses all the time—which enabled me to be there with Soft Works at the right time. As Pasteur noted, "Chance favors the prepared mind."

Even if you don't invent a product, you can still make handsome profits by getting a piece of a major deal. The classic example is Bill Gates and Microsoft.

Bill Gates became the richest man in the world, and Microsoft the richest company in the world, based on the success of its operating systems, first MS-DOS, and then the Windows series.

What put Bill Gates on the map was when IBM, then the premier manufacturer of personal computers, chose MS-DOS as the operating system for its PCs.

But Bill Gates and Microsoft didn't invent MS-DOS. A Seattle programmer, Tim Paterson, had written a personal-computer operating system called QDOS.

When Gates met with IBM, they told him they were looking for an operating system for their new PC. Gates said he had one he could sell them—but he didn't.

After his meeting with IBM, Gates went to Paterson and bought all rights to the QDOS operating system for a flat sum of $50,000, which must have seemed like a fortune to Paterson at the time. Then Microsoft renamed the system MS-DOS, made some improvements, and sold it to IBM.

And that's where Gates made his fortune. Unlike Paterson, he didn't sell MS-DOS to IBM outright. Instead, he licensed it to IBM, telling them: "For every IBM PC in which you install MS-DOS, pay us forty dollars."

Billions of dollars later, Microsoft Windows is the leading personal-computer operating system in the world, and Bill Gates is rich beyond the dreams of avarice.

HOW TO BE A BETTER NEGOTIATOR

When negotiating price, budget, project deadlines, or other numbers in a transaction, you stand a better chance of getting the other person to say yes if your proposal fits within the range that he or she has in mind. How do you find out that range? Ask.

For instance, if you are bidding on a project, ask the client, "Do you have a budget for this project?" If the client's answer is "yes," ask, "Would you mind sharing the budget figure with me?"

Usually, the other person will give it to you. Suppose the client says the budget for the project is $100,000. You now know that a bid of $95,000 will probably be accepted, but bidding $115,000 may price you out of the job.

If the client says there isn't a budget yet, ask, "Do you at least have a dollar figure in mind of what you'd like it to cost?" Often, a person who has not created a formal budget can and will answer that question.

Before you begin to negotiate, you should have the following three figures or positions fixed firmly in your mind.

- The maximum: the highest figure, the most you dare ask for without fear of "blowing away" the other party.
- The minimum: the bottom line, the lowest figure you'd settle for.
- The goal: a realistic figure that you have a good

chance of getting, probably between 50 and 75 percent of the maximum.

If you have been given the budget, propose a figure that falls within the budget. If there is no budget, start by quoting the maximum figure. Always start high. It is much easier to start high and back down than to start low and build up.

It pays to be optimistic and aim high when setting your maximum. For example, a researcher requesting funds to purchase a new piece of laboratory equipment might be able to buy an adequate machine for between $15,000 and $50,000.

If she proposes $50,000, and management cuts her budget in half, she will end up with a $25,000 machine. But by setting her initial request 20 percent higher, at $60,000, a cut in half would leave her with $30,000—and a machine with $5,000 more in capabilities and performance.

When negotiating, try for your goal, but be prepared to accept any offer between the minimum and the maximum. In some cases, you may be surprised to find that the maximum is approved without argument. At other times, the other party may not even grant you the minimum. If this happens, you may be forced to consider more drastic action, such as going to the other person's supervisor or making it a public issue in a team meeting.

8

Complacency is the death of success.

Successful businesspeople are rarely content with the status quo. They are constantly driven to greater levels of productivity and achievement.

A recent online survey, The Entrepreneur Test, identified five key characteristics most frequently possessed by successful entrepreneurs. Leading the list was "drive," which included both initiative and vigor.

As we've mentioned, one of Bo's most famous cases—the one that not only made his reputation but meant the most to him personally—was the 1981 rape and mutilation of a Roman Catholic nun in the Convent of Our Lady of Mt. Carmel Parish in Harlem.

Horrible beyond description, this heinous act offended not

only Bo Dietl, but also virtually everyone in the city. The nun was raped, sodomized, and mutilated, with the perpetrators carving twenty-seven crosses on her body with a blade. Mayor Ed Koch called it "the most vicious crime in New York City history."

"Lots of cops wanted a piece of these guys," said Bo. Though not originally assigned to the case, he demanded that his commanding officers assign him and his partner to it.

He was given permission to work on the case, but only for three days. That's when Bo and his partner, Tommy, went to work with a vengeance.

Working twenty-four hours a day for three straight days, Bo pursued leads, questioned street contacts, and interviewed hundreds of people in pursuit of the rapists. His relentless investigation led to the arrest of one male in Chicago and another in New York City.

■   ■   ■

We got a tip that one of the perpetrators had gotten out of New York City and taken a bus to Chicago. We wanted to fly out there immediately and got permission from the captain to do so, but had difficulty getting a plane because of an air traffic controllers strike.

I called the Chicago Police Department and got through to a sergeant. I told him the story; he was familiar with the nun rape case, which had made the national news. I asked him, "Sergeant, when this guy gets off the bus, can you hold him for me until my partner and I get there?" He said he would.

When I got to Chicago, the sergeant told me, "We got your man, Bo, and he already confessed doing the rape to us."

The perpetrator told us who his accomplice was, and that guy was still in Harlem. Tommy and I went to his apartment building. Tommy guarded the front door while I went up the fire escape. As I climbed, I saw him coming out of his apartment window, trying to escape.

When we took him down to the precinct and interrogated him, he was tough and surly with us. He told me he wanted to f— my mother. I told him, "You don't even know my mother," and punched him in the mouth, breaking his jaw. He sued me for forty million dollars, but nothing came of it and, of course, he was convicted and jailed.

■   ■   ■

There's an old saying: "When the going gets tough, the tough get going." A recent example from one of my case files at BDA shows how making the extra effort can produce success where others fail.

A woman in Brooklyn met a Turkish guy and was shacking up with him. She got pregnant, and they had a son. They still live together with the boy, but the Turk becomes an abusive husband, hitting her, and beating her, and breaking her leg. He was a real animal—a scumbag.

Seven years later, the Turkish guy decided that he wanted his son to live in Turkey and be the Son of Allah or some shit like that. He dragged the kid to the airport, and the wife was with them, and he got the kid aboard a flight to Turkey, where he arranged for his relatives to take the boy and raise him to be a Turk or whatever.

She cried, pleaded, begged, "Please don't take my son away from me!" She really loved this kid. But the husband didn't care. The kid got on the plane; the plane took off. The Turk tells her, "You will never see your son again."

She went to the police—the six-two precinct in Brooklyn—for help. They told her, "There's nothing we can do." She was about to leave, despondent. But as she was turning to go, one of the cops said, "There's a guy you should see, Bo Dietl. He knows everything. He can help you."

She came to my office. We mainly do corporate work, but I hate a bully, and this Turk was a bully, and she was the victim, so I agreed to take her case.

I sent two of my best men, Jimmy the Wags and Danny Cavallo, to Istanbul to recover the kid. They told me, "Bo, if we get caught, we'll get eight years in jail for this."

That's when I tapped into my network.

I called Frank Bolles, a top hostage negotiator. I told him I needed his help, and he said, "Bo, whatever you need, you got it."

I asked Frank if he had ever done any work in Turkey. It turned out he knews the Chief of Police there. And I knew that was my in. I call the Chief of Police in Istanbul, and as soon as I mentioned Frank, he was friendly and cooperative. I explained my problem and asked for his help. He said, "No problem."

I told Jimmy and Danny, "Go to the Chief of Police and put $1,500 in cash on his desk. Then wait for him to bring you the boy. When the boy is in your hands, give him another $1,500."

Within two hours, Jimmy and Danny were on a plane, flying home with the boy. His mother was crying, thanking me; she was so happy. Then the boy got off the plane, ran straight toward me, and began hitting, scratching, and cursing me. Apparently, when he was in Turkey, they told him I was some kind of white devil!

Being proactive and aggressive gives you an incredible advantage in business, because most of the people you compete with are not.

Laziness is at the base of human nature. Most people in any situation are simply not effective because they don't do what is required; they are too lazy.

My distaste for laziness and complacency intensified during my years on the police force.

Civil service is the worst. Seventy-five percent of civil servants are useless in the workplace. They do nothing; they do as little as they can get away with; they don't care. In the private sector, maybe 25 percent of people are do-nothings, so the competition is a little tougher there.

To gain the edge, it's not enough just to be good at what you do: In today's fast-paced world, you have to be just as fast.

When I was assigned routine tasks as a trainee cop—such as taking calls, dispatching police cars, whatever—I did my job as fast as I could. We would often get a backlog of calls coming in. I would tell the officers on patrol, "Stay off the air," so I could dispatch the jobs to them, which in some cases could be a matter of life or death. A backlog of calls that took other dispatchers a morning or an afternoon to get through, I could clean up in an hour.

How to Get out of a Rut at Work

Okay. Let's say you think you're suffering from job burnout—either a mild case or a severe form. You know you have a problem. What do you do about it? Here are ten suggestions—ten ways to avoid and overcome job burnout:

1) Ask for more work. Not getting a chance to work to your full potential is one of the biggest reasons for job burnout.

Why don't managers delegate more to their staffs? One reason is that they never learned how: Most managers in industry started as engineers, accountants, or in other specialized professions; they are doers, not delegators. Another is that a poor manager makes himself feel more important by hogging all the work and leaving staffers in the dark.

Working under a manager who refuses to delegate makes people feel frustrated and useless. If you're not being used to your full potential, *ask for more work.* Tell your supervisor that you can tackle more . . . and that you *want* to tackle more.

If your manager replies, "But I'm not sure you can handle more," you say, "I'll *prove* I can." Tell your manager to increase your workload just a little bit at first. Once he sees how efficiently and quickly you complete the assignment, your boss will be happy to give you as much as you can handle.

Unfortunately, some managers are never going to delegate. If you're stuck working for one of these monsters, changing jobs may be your only way out. (We'll take a look at that option a little later.)

2) *Take on different work.* People joke about being stuck in a rut. But it's no joke. One business executive I know defines a rut as "a grave without a cover."

Life shouldn't be a grind. It should be enjoyable, fun . . . even thrilling.

So if you feel stuck in a rut, get out. Break your daily routine by doing something new. For example, if you've always wanted to write but never tried to do it, volunteer to write an article for your company newsletter or a trade journal. If you've always thought sales would be fun but never tried it, volunteer to staff the booth at your company's next trade show exhibit. If you're interested in computers but haven't had much chance to work with them, take an introductory course in programming.

3) *Learn something new.* Some people end up spending their professional lives rehashing and reworking the same limited bits of knowledge they picked up in school and in their early training. For instance, one advertising writer complained to me that because he had become a specialist in automobiles, he had essentially written and rewritten the same set of ads for a dozen different clients over the course of his twenty-five-year career.

Of course, he could have broken out of this at any time. He could have studied a new area, such as consumer electronics or soap or medical products. But he didn't. And the longer he stayed within the narrow confines of automotive copywriting, the harder it became for him to try anything new.

Life and work become dull when you stop learning. So don't stop. Make it a point to broaden your knowledge, master new skills, and learn new things. For example, instead of throwing away college catalogs and course solicitations that you receive in the mail, sign up for a course in a new topic that interests you. Or, if you don't have time for night school, you can read a book, attend a lecture, or study a paper.

Rehashing the same database of knowledge you've always carried around in your brain is safe and easy. But it's also boring and can lead to job burnout. When you're continually learning new things about your work, you keep the interest and excitement level high.

4) Do something new. Go on a cruise. Learn to play the electric guitar. Build a cedar closet. It doesn't have to be work-related. The simple act of doing something *new* will boost your spirits and give you a new outlook on life—a positive attitude that will spill over into your job.

By continually trying new things, you will become well rounded. And well-rounded people are the most content, personally and professionally.

5) Become more active in your own field. Somewhere along the way, you may have lost the zest for your trade, profession, or business that you had when you first started. The daily grind of nine-to-five has worn you down.

You can escape job burnout by rekindling your interest in your profession. Join your professional society, if you haven't already. Become active: Attend meetings, read journals, present papers—you can even run for office in your local chapter. Take a course or teach one. Take responsibility for training one of the younger employees in your department. The people who are active in their field are usually the most successful and the most satisfied with their careers.

6) Restructure your job. A secretary at an advertising agency explained the source of her career blues: "I took a secretarial-level job to get my foot in the door in the advertising business. But, although this is my first job in advertising, I have a pretty extensive writing background—mainly in employee communications for several large firms.

"I thought that in an ad agency I'd get an opportunity to put my writing skills to use. But it hasn't worked out that way. I *know* I could write good copy if given a chance. But my boss thinks of me as strictly a secretary, and he has never given me the opportunity to try my hand at an ad or commercial."

Perhaps you, too, have been forced into a role against your will. Maybe you had hopes of doing creative, exciting, or challenging work but found yourself handling dry, routine procedures day after day. If you're unhappy with your job as it is, you can solve the problem by redefining your role in the organization.

First, look for opportunities: things that need doing but aren't being done. Then volunteer to take on this work.

For example, let's say you're a technical manager who would rather be doing something else, such as computer programming. If your company needs to develop a new website and you're skilled in HTML, you could take responsibility for designing the site. As your company's online presence grows, more and more of your time could be devoted to managing the website. By satisfying a need, you've also restructured your job to suit your tastes.

Of course, you can't always write your own job description. Some bosses won't allow it. And neither will some corporate structures. If that's the case, more drastic action may be needed to get your career back on track.

7) *Attack the problem head-on.* "All this sounds nice but not realistic," you may be complaining. "My problem is much more difficult than that."

Fine. Then you need to assess the source of your job burnout and attack it head-on.

For example, maybe your life is being made miserable by a coworker who refuses to cooperate with you. The two of you are supposed to be working on some of the same projects, sharing information and ideas. But your "partner" is a loner who gives you the cold shoulder whenever you try to get together.

Confrontation is unpleasant, so you could remain silent and try to make the best of it. But you won't be solving the problem; you'll just be running away. And you'll only grow more miserable as that bad situation stays bad.

The better tactic is to confront the uncooperative coworker head-on. Tell your coworker that you have a problem you want to discuss in private. Then tell him your feelings: that you want to do a good job but can't unless the two of you can find a way to work together productively and without friction. Be direct. Say, "It seems that whenever I approach you, you're not available. Have I done something to make you not want to work with me? Is there a way we can get together on this?"

In many cases, the source of our unhappiness at work is another person—a person who is making life difficult for us. By confronting difficult people with the fact that they *are* being difficult, you force them to admit their poor behavior and take steps to correct it, making life easier for everyone.

8) *Change departments.* Sometimes the person creating the problem for you *can't* be made to change. Or there may not be another job or task in your department that can provide you with career satisfaction. In that case, changing departments may be the answer.

This is a fairly common occurrence in industry. For example, an engineer who would rather deal with people than equations can move into technical sales. Or a telecommunications analyst who is bored with phones but fascinated by computers might switch to the IT department.

9) *Change employers.* If there's no place in your company where you'd be happy, then maybe you should change companies. The unfortunate fact of professional life is that many companies *are* bad to work at, many bosses *are* tyrants, and many companies *are* poorly managed (although most aren't).

If you're in one of these places, the best thing you can do is get out. By all means, keep your job-hunting a secret. And don't quit your present job until you get a new one.

On the other hand, don't rush your résumé to the printer at the first sign of trouble. Changing jobs is a major step. Are you sure your problem can't be solved by less drastic measures, such as a change of assignment, a heart-to-heart talk with your boss, or a week's vacation? Try to make things work. Only when you're convinced that you can't improve your present situation should you put yourself back on the job market.

10) *Change fields.* Changing careers is an effective cure for severe job burnout. If you've had it with what you do for a living, maybe you should do something else.

There are a number of reasons why people hesitate to choose this option. One is the feeling that they studied for a specific career, so they'd be wasting their education if they moved into a field for which they were not formally trained. But that's faulty reasoning. The real and tragic waste is working at a job that no longer fulfills you.

The second reason is financial. People worry that they'll have to take a severe pay cut when they switch fields, because they'll be starting over at entry level. But that's not always the case. True, you may not make as much as you're making now. But you'll probably earn enough to maintain your present lifestyle. If not, your savings can see you through for the year or two that it takes to reach a respectable salary in your new profession.

The third factor is that people fear radical change. But the change doesn't have to be radical; it can, in fact, be small. For example, a technical writer who is sick and tired of turning out operating manuals doesn't have to join the circus to find happiness. Maybe a different type of writing—say, newspaper reporting—will be enough of a change to break his career doldrums.

The decision to change jobs or professions should be made only after a lot of careful thought and soul-searching. But change is called for when you're stuck with a bad case of job burnout. After all, you spend more than a third of your waking hours at your job. Doesn't it make sense to have a job that you like? As an old Scottish proverb advises: "Be happy while you're living, for you're a long time dead."

9

Help people and they will help you— most of the time.

People who know me also know that they can count on me to help them out if they get into a jam. They know that if they have a problem, I will help, because I protect the people I care about.

A famous New York real estate developer was having a problem with his partner, concerning the sale of a building they owned together. The partner was approached illegally about selling the building, and the information he disclosed to the potential buyer was detrimental to the developer's liquidation of his share of the asset.

I stepped in and helped the two of them work it out without getting expensive lawyers or the courts involved. In return, the developer made me a lifetime member of two golf courses that he owns.

Another time, a casino owner was facing a class-action lawsuit accusing him of illegal activities of which he was innocent. I brought him and the lawyer for the class-action suit together, and settled it without anyone getting bloody. And what did I get in return? I developed a strong personal relationship with the casino owner. He frequently speaks before large groups, and whenever he does and I am in the area where he is speaking, he always praises me and my character in front of the audience.

I don't do these things for any reason other than to help people who need it. I truly like to help people. If you go into life and look for a payback every time you help someone, you won't be successful. I have close relationships with dozens of powerful and influential people, and most of them do not give me business, and I don't want them to. All I want from them is their friendship.

If you receive a favor, you should reciprocate because you want to and because it's the right thing to do, not because the other party demands or expects it of you. Failure to reciprocate shows a lack of gratitude and respect.

One ex-cop I knew was looking to get into a cushy private security job to make some serious money. I arranged for him to get an interview with a major corporation for a position as head of security; the pay was more than $300,000 a year. I pushed hard for him to get the job, spoke to the company's CEO, who is a friend of mine, and the cop got hired for $460,000 a year. About a year ago, when things were a little slow for us at Beau Dietl & Associates, I called him up and said, "Things are a little slow; how about throwing some work our way?"

The security chief said sure, why not? But then I never heard from him again. And I won't forget that anytime soon.

If someone does you a favor, you should do them a favor in return if and when they ask for your help. That guy is going to be looking for another security job at some point in his career, and when he is, I guarantee you he will come to me. When he does, I will remind him of what happened when I asked him to do us a favor after we had gotten him his last job, and then throw him out of my office.

But here's the key: Help people just for the sake of helping them. Do not expect or ask for any reward.

I help all kinds of people all the time. I'm always the helper, not the helpee, and I don't look for anything in return. However, if a situation comes up in which I do need their help, and they don't give it to me—well, that's something I will remember for a long time.

I'm not shy about asking for what I want. When I read in *The Wall Street Journal* that a corporation has a problem, I pick up the phone and call the chief executive, always preferring to start at the top.

When you are a friend to others, they want to be a friend to you. When you help others, they naturally want to return the favor. But it's an unspoken obligation. If you state that you are looking for something in return as you grant a favor, it destroys its effectiveness.

I must be good at giving, because when I turned fifty, three of my closest friends—my real estate partner, Steve Witkoff; Danny

DelGiorno; and Sheldon Brody—gave *me* an extraordinary gift: a birthday party at Cipriani's that cost them $650,000.

It was an unbelievable night that I will never forget. Entertainment was provided by Paul Anka and a twenty-eight-piece orchestra, flown in specifically for the occasion. Anka wrote and sang a special birthday song for me (see page 175). As the orchestra played, acrobats from Cirque du Soleil soared overhead.

More than 450 of my friends, associates, colleagues, and clients turned out for the birthday bash, including Donald Trump, Jack Welch, and Dick Grasso.

10

Communicate so that others can't help but pay attention to you.

When Bob and I first started working on this book, he had some questions, so naturally, he e-mailed them to me.

Within seconds, I had him on the phone.

"Listen," I told him, "I'm not such a big e-mail guy, so it's better if we talk in person."

Too many businesspeople hide behind e-mail and voice mail, as if they are afraid of contact with other people. Often the excuse given is, "I'm too busy to talk on the phone or meet with you in person." And how many times have you sent an e-mail to someone mainly because you didn't feel like talking to him or her?

The problem is that the busier people are, and the more important they are, the easier it is for them to ignore you.

A case in point: A pharmaceutical industry trade association, the Pharmaceutical Research and Manufacturers of America (PhRMA), began a national campaign to stop the importation of drugs from Canada and other countries into the United States. While the imports naturally cut into the revenues of American pharmaceutical firms, there are other problems with importing prescription drugs. The quality and ingredients of these drugs are often questionable. There is an ongoing fear that terrorists could contaminate the prescription drugs with the smallpox virus or anthrax. Online marketers of prescription drugs from overseas often sell the drugs without a prescription from the patient's doctor; these prescriptions are issued by doctors who are paid by the online marketers—and they write the prescriptions without examining the patients.

PhRMA had hired another investigator to report on the problems of importing prescription drugs from overseas. They charged something like a million dollars for an investigative report.

It was a great report, no doubt about it. There was only one problem—no one in the government would read it!

Here's where I applied the principles of what I call "shock therapy"—making your message stand out from the glut of other information your audience has to deal with, making sure it is delivered to their desk, and then making sure they read it.

Politicians supporting the import of prescription drugs held a press conference in Washington, D.C. In attendance were Reps. Gil Gutknecht, a Minnesota Republican; Bernard Sanders, a Vermont independent; and Rahm Emanuel, an Illinois Democrat; as well as Governor Rod Blagojevich of Illinois.

I burst into the room and stepped up to the podium in front

of the cameras, holding up a second investigative report, this one prepared by BDA. "You've got to read this," I told the bewildered politicians. "This is a life-or-death issue! You're going to poison half of America! All you want to do is appease the elderly vote."

The other private-investigation firm wrote a great report, but we got politicians to read ours. I flew down to Washington, D.C., every week and testified in front of the U.S. Congressional and Senate subcommittees. More important, I personally went to the offices of fifty senators and thirty congressmen, met with them, handed them the report, and said, "Read it!"

I called on media friends to help my crusade against imported pharmaceuticals. I had Tom Brokaw in my office so I could explain the importance of the report to him. I talked about the dangers of imported medications on Imus and a lot of other media, including Cramer and Kudlow.

But I didn't merely rely on the facts provided by the other investigative firm in their report. My firm, Beau Dietl & Associates, ordered more than one hundred medications from Internet pharmacies. Some of them arrived improperly packaged, from unexpected countries, or from operations run by shady characters. If Congress legalizes importation, these problems would multiply.

We placed online orders for 146 drugs and received more than fifty, even though no doctor had ever written a prescription. We sent the drugs to be tested, and preliminary results showed some contaminants.

I even had my kids, who were nine and thirteen at the time, order prescription medications online. Of course, it is illegal to sell prescription medications to minors. My daughter Dana was able to order a weight-loss drug that is on the Drug Enforcement Agency's list of controlled substances. My son received a shipment of Prozac, even though he disclosed that he was only four feet eight inches tall and weighed seventy pounds.

As good as the other firm's investigative report was, I felt it needed more, so I sent my own investigators overseas. One picture is worth a thousand words, so I wanted to add some photographic evidence to the report in the packets I handed out on Capitol Hill. Pictures get people's attention and make your evidence much more believable.

One of the surveillance photos shows a New Jersey physician who writes prescriptions for online customers he never meets. Another shot, taken by a BDA operative in Kashmir, showed a dusty truck transporting medications to be shipped to U.S. consumers who ordered them online.

My employees have checked out more than 1,400 websites that advertise low-priced medicines, especially from Canadian pharmacies. We ordered and received pills prescribed by doctors unknown to any of us. Those doctors never talked to us and, of course, never examined us.

According to Elizabeth Willis, chief of the drug operation section of the DEA's office of division control, "If a prescription is written by a doctor based solely on information from an online questionnaire, it's not valid, so the distribution is illegal."

The FDA now has ninety different Internet drug investigations under way, according to a high-level agency official. By making it easy to order drugs online without a prescription, these

Internet sites are contributing to the growing drug problem in the United States.

For instance, abuse of prescription painkillers is soaring. In 2002, 22 percent of people ages eighteen to twenty-five abused prescription pain pills, up from 7 percent in 1992. A survey of emergency-room visits found that painkiller abuse nearly tripled from 1994 to 2002 and is now as common as abuse of heroin or marijuana.

Many PR firms hired to publicize such a report would hold a press conference, but as far as I know, I'm the only guy who would storm into the other side's press conference to get my message heard.

We have children using their parents' credit cards to order medicine that is on the FDA's Import Alert List or the DEA's Controlled Substance list. We have senior citizens who are willing to jeopardize their own lives by buying their medicine from these sites because they want to save a few dollars, which is why politicians who want the senior vote support this bill. We have teenagers and college students who are heavily engaged in buying and selling these prescription drugs.

We know that counterfeit and contaminated medicines have killed people. For instance, 2,500 Nigerian children infected with meningitis died because they were taking fake medicine, and thirty-three children from India died from ingesting contaminated pills.

A guy in Illinois died of a heart attack after taking Viagra that he bought on the Internet. The son of a Georgia minister died as a result of taking pills he bought from South Africa.

Both the House and the Senate were looking at bills that would allow importation of medicines by individuals under certain conditions. The House bill would permit it only when people physically bring medicine into the United States. Both bills would legalize importation by pharmacies and wholesalers if federal regulators deemed it safe, but a separate House bill would do away with safety certification. The Senate bill would permit drug imports only from Canada, while the House bill would allow imports from twenty-five countries.

Osama Bin Laden or other terrorists could use the Internet to distribute dangerous drugs to unsuspecting consumers. The gloves have to come off. This bill is going to get railroaded through.

■   ■   ■

I learned how to communicate for results during my years with the NYPD. The key: Speak clearly and directly, and sound like you mean what you say. Better yet, mean what you say.

Once, I was on a homicide investigation, and I was canvassing the area. I rang a bell, and a kid came to the door. He was about five years old, bare-assed naked, and filthy.

I asked him, "Where's your mother?" and he giggled. There were two other kids there. They were triplets. All naked. All filthy. I mean, shit all over them.

I walked into the house, and there was the mother. She was a foster mother, and got money for taking care of the kids.

I took her aside and said, "Listen, I do not see any food for the kids, and I do not see any clothes for these kids. I will be back in one week, *and let me tell you something.* If this place isn't clean, if these kids are not wearing clothes, if I do not see food, *I am taking these kids away.*"

I came back in a week, just like I promised. And the place was clean and the kids were dressed and the refrigerator was full. I kept going back there, giving the kids money, and making sure they were taken care of.

■ ■ ■

Sometimes, when I was on the force, I found that actions spoke louder than words when it came to getting the results I wanted.

A big Dutch cop, about six-foot-four, was picking on the rookies, guys who didn't yet have their gold shield. He saw to it that they caught the shit details. I said, "Let's make a chart; we all need to take a shot at the shit details."

He said, "You stay the f—k out of this."

I told him, "Hey, we're all working together. We're all cops, whether we have a silver shield or gold shield."

The Dutchman put his finger in my face and said, "You are messing with the wrong guy," and he swung a punch.

So I clobbered him . . . even though he was eight inches taller and a weight class heavier.

I was on top of him, punching him, when my lieutenant came in and yelled, "You two, into my office."

The Dutchman was standing there, blood dripping all over him. The lieutenant asked, "What happened?"

I said, "We had a slight disagreement." He told both of us to get out of his office.

The Dutch cop shook my hand and stopped picking on the rookies with the silver shields.

11

Be a tough boss, but lead by example.

There is a leadership crisis in corporate America today.

The number of CEOs ousted for poor performance has increased 130 percent over the past six years. And according to a Harris Poll, only one third of the senior management of Fortune 400 companies feel confident in the abilities of the next generation of business leaders. No wonder 40 percent of U.S. corporations now have some sort of formal leadership-training program.

Although, as the CEO of one of the nation's largest and most prestigious corporate-security firms, Bo leaves most of the day-to-day detecting to his employees, he never asks them to do anything that he would not do himself.

Shortly after 9/11, Bo was out networking one night, as he is every night, attending a party at the Delmonico Hotel, when he was interrupted by a call on his cell phone at 2 in the morning.

A client, Lehman Brothers Holding Inc., had found a suspicious-looking white powder at its facility in Jersey City, New Jersey, and was worried that it might be anthrax.

Bo left the party in Manhattan and drove out to Jersey City in his BMW to handle the matter personally, where he sealed off the building. The white powder turned out to be a harmless substance. Says Thomas Russo, a VP at Lehman, "If you have a problem, Bo's the guy to call."

As the CEO of one of the country's largest security firms, the best use of Bo's time is not field investigations; it's running the company. But one of the reasons his employees love working for Bo and follow his leadership is that they know he can do, has done, and will do everything that he asks them to do.

■   ■   ■

Four years ago, a young woman in her twenties fell out a window in Richmond, Virginia. The local police ruled it suicide and closed the case, but the parents couldn't believe it and hired us to investigate.

We went to Richmond and interviewed witnesses. One witness said she was sitting on a windowsill on a high floor of the building and fell out. I knew he was lying; her parents had told me the girl had a fear of heights. My team and I continued the investigation, plugged away at the case (which was almost three years old by the time we were brought in) for eighteen months, and as this chapter is being written, the two suspects have been arrested for murder.

The parents wanted closure, to know that their little girl had not taken her own life. Now they have it.

I am a roll-up-my-sleeves type of guy who gets things done. To be a good CEO, a good leader, you must have the respect of your people. Your people have to believe in you so that when they have a problem, and they look to you for help, they are confident that you can help them out.

Through the grapevine, I hear that my employees say they are thrilled to be working for me. Not that they should be, but that makes me feel I have to be an extra-good CEO. As a leader, you have to believe in yourself, be confident in yourself, so employees and clients can see that confidence and belief, and respect you for it.

Be realistic in your assessment of how effective you are as a leader today, and resolve to improve. There are four stages of competence in any activity, whether it's running a company, investigating homicides, or cooking a meal.

The lowest level of competence is "unconscious incompetence." You don't know what you are doing—and worse, you don't know that you don't know.

The next stage up the ladder is "conscious incompetence." You've recognized that the reason you are not successful in your endeavor is that you don't know what you're doing.

"Conscious incompetence" is better than "unconscious incompetence," because people in the former stage are amenable to guidance, while those in the latter stage are not.

Moving higher up the ladder of competence, you reach the stage of "conscious competence." You've read the books, taken the courses, had real-world experience and on-the-job training, and understand what works, what is required to get the job done. But your experience at putting it into practice is limited.

That means whenever you want to accomplish a task, you have to slow down and think about what you are doing. It doesn't come naturally.

Don't try to reinvent the wheel. Observe what works, and adapt it to your own activities. Model yourself after others who are already successful in your business or related areas.

Do this enough times, and you will slowly begin to become a true master of the task at hand. You will reach the highest level of "unconscious competence."

At this stage, doing the work is second nature to you. You do it naturally, without having to consult others. The quality of your work is better, and it comes faster and easier.

How long will it take you to become a master, to reach the level of unconscious competence as a manager, supervisor, or executive?

Entrepreneur Michael Masterson says it takes approximately one thousand hours of practice to become really competent at anything. If you have expert guidance, you may be able to cut that to five hundred hours.

But ultimately, you learn by doing—and by doing a lot. If you are at this stage, keep doing more and more of the activity or task. Remember the cabdriver who, when asked, "How do I get to Carnegie Hall?" replied, "Practice, practice, practice." When you put in five thousand hours—whether it's learning to do research online, negotiating deals, or being CEO of your own business—

you will become great, not just good, and your results will be even better.

12 TIPS FOR MOTIVATING YOUR EMPLOYEES

1. Involve employees in the decision-making process. Give employees a share in decision-making—if not deciding what is to be done, then how it is to be done or when or in what way or by whom. Let their "share" of the decision making increase over time.

2. Keep employees informed. Keep employees informed about changes that can directly affect them, such as policy changes, procedure or rule changes, product information changes, and performance changes.

3. Be aware of the morale level of your employees. Be sensitive to changes in morale. Know when and why it goes up or down.

4. Maintain an open-door policy. Be approachable, available, and interested, not distant.

5. Develop a caring attitude. A good manager trains, develops, counsels, guides, and supports his or her employees.

6. Be sure to listen. Always listen to and try to understand what employees are communicating.

7. Always treat your employees with respect. Be thoughtful and considerate of the person you are dealing with.

8. Ask for suggestions. Be sure to invite suggestions and new ideas from employees concerning work. Be willing to put good ideas into action by making changes.

9. Give "constructive" criticism. An effective manager gives constructive criticism and never makes personal attacks.

10. Recognize your employees. Give appropriate praise and recognition for a job well done.

11. Outline job responsibilities. Make certain employees know exactly what is expected of them and how their performance will be evaluated.

12. Maintain high standards. By involving employees in establishing high standards of performance, you will build their pride and self-confidence.

12

Cause people to be attracted to you.

Many self-help authors talk about the importance of having a "magnetic personality" or using the "principles of attraction." What they mean is that you should take steps to become the kind of person that people will want do business with because they are attracted by your personality.

"It's not a personality contest!" you may object. "They will choose me because my product is better."

Unfortunately for you, any experienced salesperson can tell you that this isn't so. Yes, customers want a good product at a good price. But above all else, people do business with people they like, and they don't buy from people they don't like.

So it is a popularity contest, and you are already in it. Since you've already been entered by your customers and prospects, doesn't it make sense to win?

When I first met Bo, it was glaringly obvious that he possessed a magnetic personality. People are attracted by him, they like him, and they want to be part of his circle.

Some people have such attractive personalities that it makes others *want to do business with them*. Bo is such a person. They have a "magnetic selling personality"—meaning that people are attracted to them and want to have a professional relationship with them.

You and I may not radiate the same charisma, but there are still many things we can do to increase our ability to attract others to us.

All of us are born with a certain quantity of charisma, but most of what you need to increase your ability to attract prospects to you magnetically can be learned and developed over time.

■　　　■　　　■

So, what gives me my so-called "magnetic personality"? Whatever it is that makes me me, I can think of ten factors that can help draw people to you.

First, people tend to do business with people they like. So behave in a way that makes you likable. Be polite and patient. Avoid being crude, rude, gruff, or impatient—that sort of thing.

Now, anyone who knows me knows that on the rarest of rare occasions, I've been known to use colorful language, including profanity. Who am I kidding? That's complete bullshit—I curse like a sailor, and I can get away with it, because people know I was a street cop in New York City, so they accept the way I speak.

Some even find it charming. That said, unless you've got a *One Tough Cop* persona that people already accept, dropping f-bombs and crapping all over the language has the potential to turn people off, so don't f—ing do it.

Second, people are attracted to people who keep their word. So, when you make a promise, do exactly what you promised by the deadline you promised—or sooner.

I do what I say I will do. And I usually do it faster than you would expect. I get results, so people trust me.

Third, people are attracted to people whom they believe have their best interests at heart. They know that you have their best interests at heart when they hear you give them advice that benefits them the most, in spite of the fact that you won't make any money by doing so.

I have literally hundreds, perhaps thousands, of contacts in my Rolodex. They know that if they need something, I'm the guy to go to; I'll come through for them. And as a result, they come through for me.

Fourth, people are attracted to people who they believe are experts in their fields—the "gurus." To use this principle, first actually *become* a leading expert in your field through practice, research, training, education, and study.

My field is security, and everything I did for the NYPD, every ounce of fame and recognition I scrapped, makes a natural connection for anyone looking for security and investigative work.

Then, do things—such as writing articles and books or giving speeches—that demonstrate your expertise to others, including potential customers. In my case, I wrote a book about my exploits, *One Tough Cop*, which was then made into a movie. And now I've written another book—the one you are reading now.

Fifth, people are attracted to people who are honest, ethical, and aboveboard. Why lie in your marketing and elsewhere, when telling the truth is so much more effective at getting you the business?

When I was a street cop for the NYPD, I worked plenty of cases involving abused, neglected, or abandoned kids. My lieutenants told me: Forget about it; looking after these kids isn't in your job description; you're supposed to be a detective. "I'm sorry, but first I am supposed to be a human being," was my response.

Sixth, people are attracted to people who are physically attractive, or at least not physically repulsive. In chapter 1, you learned the lengths I take to maintain my appearance—fitness, exercise, dress, and grooming—to radiate an attractive physical image.

Eat right. Exercise. Stay fit. Be well-groomed. Dress well. Have good personal hygiene. Shower regularly. Brush your teeth and visit your dentist as needed. Being healthy and hygienic isn't the same as being vain. Know the difference.

Seventh, people are attracted to people who seem "real"— meaning they seem to be just regular people. A lot of corporate CEOs earning million-dollar salaries while their workers struggle to make ends meet don't seem like real people to us. But my lower-middle-class upbringing and career as a police officer make me about as "real" as you can get, as far as my employees and associates are concerned.

Be cordial, friendly, and interested in others. The best way to establish rapport and begin a relationship is to ask the other person questions—about his or her company, job, industry, even family and interests.

It's so easy. And it's extremely effective, because very few people use this technique. (Most people prefer to just talk about themselves, and indulge in this desire at every opportunity.)

Eighth, people are attracted to people who listen—and who really hear what they are saying. Remember the old saying: You have two ears and one mouth, so you should listen twice as much as you talk.

Actually, for best results, you should spend 80 percent of any conversation listening, and talk only 20 percent of the time. I love to talk, but don't be fooled. I hear what other people are saying.

Ninth, people are attracted to people who are like them. The trick here is to establish one thing that you have in common with the other person—golf, kids, pets, etc.—and allow that to grow and cement the bond between you.

I network to build my business interests. I believe that when you have a large network, you can get things done much faster and easier than those who approach potential clients, partners, and employers as strangers.

Tenth, people are attracted to other people (as well as companies and products) that make their lives easier and save them time. They also prefer to deal with people who are flexible and accommodating, not rigid and difficult. And they hate it when you waste their time, although they are not terribly concerned about wasting yours.

Bottom line: Practice these ten techniques (or traits, or whatever you want to call them) until they come as naturally and easily as driving a car or tying your shoe. When you do, you will attract at least twice as many prospects, close at least twice as many deals, and earn at least twice the income you are making today.

6 WAYS TO IMPROVE YOUR LISTENING SKILLS

To develop a magnetic personality, you've got to be a good listener; people are attracted to others who show a genuine interest in them and their needs. Here are six tips for improving your listening skills.

1. Don't talk. Listen. Studies show that job applicants are more likely to make a favorable impression and get a job offer when they let the interviewer do most of the talking. This demonstrates that people appreciate a good listener more than they do a good talker.

Why is this so? Because people want a chance to get their own ideas and opinions across. A good listener lets them do it. If you interrupt the speaker or put limitations on your listening time, the speaker will get the impression that you're not interested in what he is saying—even if you are. So be courteous and give the speaker your full attention.

This technique can help you win friends, supporters, and sales. Says top salesman Frank Bettger, "I no longer worry about being a brilliant conversationalist. I simply try to be a good listener. I notice that people who do that are usually welcome wherever they go."

2. Don't jump to conclusions. Many people tune out a speaker when they think they have the gist of his or her conversation or know what the speaker is trying to say next. But assumptions can be dangerous. Maybe the speaker is not following the same train of thought that you are, or is not planning to make the point you think he is. If you don't listen, you may miss the real point that the speaker is trying to get across.

3. Listen "between the lines." Concentrate on what is not being said as well as what is being said. Remember, a lot of clues to meaning come from the speaker's tone of voice, facial expressions, and gestures. People don't always say what they mean, but their body language is usually an accurate indication of their attitude and emotional state.

4. Ask questions. If you are not sure of what the speaker is saying, ask. It's perfectly acceptable to say, "Do you mean . . . ?" or "Did I understand you to say . . . ?" It's also a good idea to repeat what the speaker has said in your own words to confirm that you have understood him or her correctly.

Sometimes we cling to the mistaken notion that we are supposed to know everything. However, with the explosion of technology and information, that's impossible. As Thomas Edison said, "We don't know one millionth of one percent about anything." The only way you learn is by listening and asking questions.

5. Don't let yourself be distracted by the environment or by the speaker's appearance, accent, mannerisms, or word use. It's sometimes difficult to overlook a strong accent, a twitch, sexist language, a fly buzzing around the speaker's head, or similar distractions. But paying too much attention to these distractions can break your concentration and make you miss the point of the conversation.

If outside commotion is a problem, try to position yourself away from it. Make eye contact with the speaker and force yourself to focus on the message, not the environment.

And keep an open mind. Don't just listen for statements that back up your own opinions and support your beliefs, or for certain parts that interest you. The point of listening, after all, is to gain new information.

Be willing to listen to someone else's point of view and ideas. A subject that may seem boring or trivial at first can turn out to be fascinating, if you listen with an open mind.

Also, take advantage of your brain power. On the average, you can think four times faster than the speaker can talk. So, when listening, use this extra brainpower to evaluate what has been said and summarize the central ideas in your own mind. That way, you'll be better prepared to answer any questions or criticisms that the speaker poses, and you'll be able to discuss the topic much more effectively.

6. Provide feedback. Make eye contact with the speaker. Show him that you understand what he is saying by nodding your head, maintaining an upright posture, and, if appropriate, interjecting an occasional comment such as "I see" or

"That's interesting" or "Really?" The speaker will appreciate your interest and will know that you are really listening.

Motivation is an essential key to becoming a good listener. Think how your ears perk up if someone says, "Let me tell you how pleased I am with that report you did," or "I'm going to reorganize the department, and you are in line for a promotion."

To get the most out of a meeting, speech, or conversation, go in with a positive attitude. Ask yourself, *What can I learn from this to make me more valuable in my industry and to my company?* You might be surprised at what you can learn, even from routine meetings and bull sessions at the water fountain.

13

Have a unique selling proposition (USP).

Security and investigations are the primary activities of Beau Dietl & Associates, and it's an extremely competitive business. The same can be said for almost every industry on the planet—from advertising and accounting to dry cleaning, landscaping, and video rentals.

So how do you stand out from the crowd? By having your own USP—unique selling proposition.

As any marketing professional worth his salt knows, the USP is what makes your product, service, or company different—the distinguishing factor that makes you stand out from the many other businesses in the same line of work as you are.

In 1961, Rosser Reeves published his classic book, *Reality in Advertising*, in which he introduced the notion of the USP. Today, the book is out of print and difficult to get. As a result, most businesspeople haven't read it and don't know the original definition of USP. Their lack of knowledge often produces USPs that are weak and ineffective.

According to Reeves, there are three requirements for a USP (the text in italics was taken directly from *Reality in Advertising*):

1. *Each advertisement must make a proposition to the consumer. Each must say, "Buy this product, and you will get this specific benefit."*

Your headline must contain a benefit—a promise to the reader. "Promise, large promise, is the soul of an advertisement," says Samuel Johnson.

Reeves and Johnson were talking about ads, but the USP applies to any sales and marketing situation—any situation in which you have to convince a potential client to hire you instead of your competitors.

Think of the headline as the first page of your proposal, the first five seconds of your TV commercial, the front cover of your company's brochure, the copy at the top of your website home page, the first fifteen seconds of your telemarketing script, the first one minute of your sales presentation.

You must lead off with a compelling reason why the prospect should buy your product or service instead of another. You must tell him or her the benefit of hiring you—how the prospect will come out ahead by engaging your services or installing your product.

2. *The proposition must be one that the competition either cannot, or does not, offer. It must be unique—either a uniqueness of brand or a claim not otherwise made in the field.*

Here's where the "unique" in unique selling proposition comes into play. It is not enough merely to offer a benefit. You must also *differentiate* your product. "You have to have something unique you can put on the table when you are in a meeting," says Bo.

For most small businesses, the differentiating proposition is a claim not otherwise made in the field. For example, I asked Bo what the USP was for Beau Dietl & Associates. He replied, "We do twice as good a job as the other security firms at half the cost." That's a clear differentiating factor, logical and easy to remember.

Bo says that the second part of BDA's USP is, "We offer a fuller range of security services than any other security firm" (see the appendix for a listing of BDA's various services).

The third part of BDA's USP is that it can offer this broader spectrum of service because its employees have a broader spectrum of experience. When you call on BDA, you access a pool of talent experienced in everything from rescuing kidnapped children to forensic computer searches.

The BDA website (www.beaudietl.com) says: "What differentiates our company from others in the investigative arena is one word: experience. Prompt turnaround, quality investigations, and continuing communication make BDA the benchmark for excellence in investigations."

For big corporations, the differentiating proposition is a uniqueness of brand, a brand awareness built up by millions or billons of dollars spent on national advertising campaigns.

For instance, if you want a cola, you can get one from many different manufacturers: Pepsi, Coca-Cola, RC Cola, and half a dozen other brands. But if you want a "Coke," because advertising has stimulated your awareness and built your preference for this brand, you can get it from only one company: Coca-Cola.

I tend to think part of Bo's USP is a service proposition—"twice the service at half the cost"—but that his real USP lies with the Bo Dietl brand.

When you hire a security firm, you have a choice of a number of companies. But if you want the famous and decorated NYPD officer Bo Dietl—if you want to hire One Tough Cop—you can only get him at BDA.

3. The proposition must be so strong that it can move the mass millions, i.e., pull over new customers to your product.

The differentiation cannot be trivial. It must be a difference that is very important to the customer.

Why do so many businesses fail? One reason is that the marketers have not formulated a strong USP for the products and built advertising upon it.

Formulating a USP isn't difficult, but it does take some thinking; and many people don't like to think. But when you start creating a sales and marketing program without first thinking about what your USP is, your marketing will be weak because there is nothing in it to compel the customer to respond. It looks and sounds like everyone else, and what it says isn't important to the customer.

In general advertising for packaged goods, marketers achieve differentiation by building a strong brand at a cost of millions or even billions of dollars.

As we said, Coca-Cola has an advantage because of its brand. If you want a cola, you can get it from a dozen soda makers. But if you want a Coke, you can get it only from Coca-Cola.

Intel has achieved a similar brand dominance, at an extraordinary cost, with its Pentium line of semiconductors.

Most small businesses have too strong a need to generate an immediate positive return on investment to engage in this kind of expensive brand building. So we use other means to achieve the differentiation in our USP.

One option is to build your brand, fame, and visibility through low-cost publicity rather than expensive advertising, as Bo Dietl has done.

Another option is to differentiate your product or service from the competition based on a feature that your product or service has and theirs doesn't.

The common error here is building the USP around a feature that while different, is unimportant to the prospect and therefore unlikely to move him or her to try your product or service.

For example, in the pump industry, it is common for pump manufacturers to attempt to win customers by advertising a unique design feature. Unfortunately, these design twists often result in no real performance improvement, no real advantage that the customer cares about.

Realizing that they could not differentiate based on a concrete design principle, Blackmer pump took a different tack: They created a USP based upon *application* of the product.

Their trade ads showed a page from the Yellow Pages ripped

out of an industrial buying guide, full of listings for pump manufacturers, including Blackmer. Their company name was circled in pen.

The headline of the ad read: "There are only certain times you should call Blackmer for a pump. Know when?"

Body copy explained (and we are paraphrasing here), "In many applications, Blackmer performs no better or worse than many other pumps, and so we are not a particularly advantageous choice."

But, the ad went on, for certain applications (viscous fluids, fluids containing abrasives, slurries, and a few other situations), Blackmer was proven to outperform all other pumps, and was the logical brand of choice. Blackmer closed the ad by offering a free technical manual proving the claim.

Jim Alexander, of Alexander Marketing in Grand Rapids, Michigan, created this campaign and reports that it worked extremely well.

The easiest situation in which to create a strong USP is when your product has a unique feature—one that the competition lacks—that delivers a strong benefit. This must be an advantage that the customer really cares about. Not one that, though a difference, is trivial.

But what if such a proprietary advantage does not exist? What if your product is basically the same as the competition, with no special features?

Reeves has the answer here, too. He said the uniqueness can stem either from a strong brand (already discussed as an option 95 percent of marketers can't use) or from "a claim not otherwise made in that particular form of advertising"—that is, other products may have this feature, too, but advertisers haven't told consumers about it.

Here's an example from packaged-goods advertising: "M&M's melt in your mouth, not in your hand."

Once M&M's established this claim as their USP, what could the competition do? Run an ad that said, "We *also* melt in your mouth, not in your hand!"?

In his book *Scientific Advertising*, Claude Hopkins gives an example of a USP that has become a classic story. The short version: An ad man who was walking through his beer client's brewery was fascinated by a machine that blasted steam into beer bottles to sanitize them.

"Don't use that in advertising," the brewer told the ad man. "It is nothing unique; every brewer does the same."

"Maybe," the ad man replied, "but I had never heard of it before, and neither has any of the beer-drinking public."

He then created a successful ad campaign for a beer advertised as "So pure, the bottles are washed in live steam."

"You have to have something unique you can bring to the table," says Bo. "That's why having a USP is so critical."

Trust him on this. Remember, Bo knows.

HOW TO PRICE YOUR SERVICES

One of the toughest questions beginning *and* experienced service providers wrestle with is: "How much should I charge?"

You probably have a standard fee, or range of fees, that you want to charge (or have been charging) your clients. But is it the *right* fee? The amount of money you charge and how you present this fee to your potential clients play a big role in determining whether you make the sale and get the project.

Charge too *little,* and you diminish your prestige and importance in the eyes of your client. You also diminish the perceived value of your services and dramatically reduce your own earnings.

A low fee may get you a contract that you might otherwise have lost, but will you be happy doing the work for so little money?

People who sell products don't worry about this too much, because they can usually make it up in volume. But when you are selling your services, you are also selling the finite amount of time that you have available to perform these services. In fact, time is your only moneymaking resource, and there's a sharply limited inventory. So you can't afford to give your time away too cheaply.

On the other hand, charge *too much* and you may price yourself out of the market, losing out on jobs to other service providers who charge less.

Because each industry is different, we can't go into a comparison of the hourly rates or project fees that others typically charge in your profession or trade, or how clients or customers in your market are billed, or give a detailed course on cost estimating for each type of service. If you've been in business for any length of time, you already know these things about your own industry.

But we do want to ensure that you charge your clients competitive fees. These are fees that bring you maximum revenue without causing you to lose those projects you want to get.

Here are four important factors to consider when determining what to charge your client:

1. *Your status.* Are you a beginner or an old pro? Are you well known in your field and highly recommended, or are you still waiting to be discovered by the masses? Are you a novice, learning your craft as you go, or are you really a master at what you do?

And do you just *think* you're good, or do you have the client list, testimonials, referrals, and track record to back up the big fees you want to charge?

Because of their status, experienced service providers generally can command higher fees than beginners. But ability is even more important, so a highly talented novice is worth more to clients than a hack, no matter how long the hack has been working.

As a rule, those who are less experienced set their fees at the lower end of the scale; old pros set their fees at the higher end. But be careful about underpricing yourself.

Beginners have a tendency to set their fees at the absolute bottom of the scale, reasoning that they do not have the experience or credentials to justify higher rates. However, clients will probably take you more seriously if you put your fees in the medium to medium-high range. The less a client pays for a job, the less he or she respects the work and the person who produced it.

2. The going rate for your type of service (i.e., what the market will bear). Unless you are the number-one great guru of your industry, or the most in-demand contractor in your town, your rates will have to be *somewhat* reflective of what the standard rates are for your type of service. And even if you are the great guru, there's still an upper limit to what most clients can afford or are willing to pay you.

In some industries, pricing is fairly standard. Some service fields are regulated; in others, professional societies or codes of behavior set fee guidelines. On the other hand, many businesses have no such standards, and their fees, as one professional put it, "are all over the lot."

The variation in fees in many fields is tremendous. However, by talking with a few prospects, you can quickly get a sense of the upper and lower limits of what you can charge.

You may find, for example, that some homeowners expect to pay $1,000 for landscaping, while others are willing to spend $10,000 or more. But no one expects to get it for $200, and no one is willing to go above $20,000. After a few initial conversations and meetings with potential clients, you'll get a good idea of what the market will bear.

The important thing to remember is that you are not

locked into an hourly or project rate because you quoted it to one client. You can experiment with different rates until you find the right *range* for your services and your market.

3. *The competition in your local area.* Call some of your competitors and ask them what they are charging. Many will gladly tell you. If not, you still need to get this information, so it's acceptable to do so undercover. Call or have a friend call a few of your competitors. Describe a typical project, and get a cost estimate. See if they have a published fee schedule or price list, and ask them to send you a copy.

Finding out the competition's fees is a real help in closing sales. You learn just where to price yourself in relation to other firms that offer similar services.

You'll also benefit by asking your competitors to send you their brochures and other sales materials. By reviewing these materials, you can learn much about their sales and marketing approaches.

4. *Your current financial need.* How much do you need the work and the income? In some situations, when cash flow is slow, you may feel financial pressure to get the work. At other times, you may not need the money, but psychologically, you need to close the deal in order to feel successful and good about yourself.

Your need to get the work really should not be a consideration in setting your fees. But, practically speaking, it is for most of us.

If you've got a million bucks in the bank, or if dozens of top corporations are knocking at your door, begging you to make space for their projects in your busy schedule, then obviously you don't need the work, and this helps at the bargaining table. If the job isn't right, or the prospect gives off bad vibes or haggles over your fee, you can walk away without regrets.

If, on the other hand, the rent check is three weeks overdue and you haven't had a phone call or an assignment in the past two months, you may be willing to take on a less-than-ideal project or a client who, if he senses your neediness, may use this to his advantage in price negotiations.

Ideally, you should negotiate each project as if you don't really need or want the work. But when you're hungry and/or just starting out, this isn't always possible or even wise. Sometimes you need the ego boost that comes with landing a project or being busy with work. For the service provider, "psychic," or emotional, wages can be as important as the green, folding kind.

14

Take a risk.

"Managers who consistently perform at a higher level are uniformly more comfortable taking risks than most," says Jim McCormick, a motivational speaker and national skydiving champion.

Some people are natural risk-takers: Richard Branson, Bo Dietl, Larry Ellison, and Muhammad Ali come immediately to mind.

Most of us, however, would prefer not to take risks. Fear holds us back.

"People do things out of fear," says writer Harlan Ellison. "You know what I mean: They'll lose their job, their rep will be ruined, no one will love them, their family won't be able to eat, blah, blah, blah, and those are exactly the usual fears that society uses, and has *always* used, to keep you in line, to keep you doing things you don't want to do, to shame you into political correctness and conformity, in a job you don't like, in a relationship you can't stand, terrified that if you don't worship and think exactly as you're told, you'll go to Hell or, worse, never get that autographed photo of Jerry Falwell."

Not being afraid of taking risks is a huge advantage in the business world, one Bo Dietl possesses in abundance.

There is no business school that can teach you to be more courageous or to increase your tolerance for risk-taking. The only way to overcome fear is to face what you fear and do it anyway. The only way to build up your tolerance for risk-taking is to take risks—small at first, then bigger and bigger.

Bo is no stranger to taking risks when it comes to getting results for the clients of Beau Dietl & Associates. He recalls the time a corporate VP called on him to rescue the man's two-year-old son from a kidnapper: the boy's mother.

■   ■   ■

The guy had married a Danish woman, and she didn't like living in the United States. She told him she was taking their son to visit her parents in the little town where she grew up in Denmark. A few weeks later, she called and told him, "I'm not coming back, and I'm keeping our son."

We put together a team, created a plan, and flew to Denmark. When we got there, I went to a local business office and got some papers that looked semiofficial. On the forms, we typed in words to the effect that we were authorized to bring the child back and that he was kidnapped illegally because the boy is an American citizen. The idea was that when we went to the grandparents' house to get the kid, we would show them the papers so they think we have a subpoena or something. Of course, it's not a subpoena, and the whole thing is bogus.

I needed a helicopter and pilot to fly into the village and retrieve the kid. The chopper pilot had been a Nazi fighter pilot in World War II; I told him we were shooting a new version of *The Sound of Music* and needed him to fly us over the town to check out the scenery or something. He didn't quite believe me, but I offered him a lot of money.

One of my guys, Jimmy the Wags, is a former police sergeant. He went with the boy's father and another one of my people, an ex-Army officer, to the house by car. When Jimmy knocked on the door, it opened, and there was the wife's father—the kid's grandpa—aiming a shotgun at his head.

I was in the chopper on a walkie-talkie. "Go in and get the kid, Jimmy," I told him. Looking down, I saw a white vehicle with a flashing blue light heading toward the house at high speed: The family had called the local cops.

Jimmy said, "Bo, there's a guy here with a shotgun pointed right at my head." I asked him how old the guy was. "About seventy, Bo," said Jimmy. I told Jimmy, "You're an ex–Green Beret and you're six-foot-three. Take the gun from him and get the kid," which he did.

Meanwhile, the Nazi chopper pilot saw the police on their way and refused to land so we could make the pickup. I told him to get down there and do what I paid him to do. He told me to shove it, and began rocking the copter back and forth, either to scare me or make me sick or both. I don't get scared, but I do get queasy. I got in his face and told him, "Set this chopper down now or I'll throw up all over your f—ing dashboard." I also told him that if he didn't do what I said right then, he wouldn't get the rest of his money.

That convinced him, and he brought the helicopter down. I ran out and to the front door, and we took the kid, with his Danish family screaming and the cop siren blaring in the distance, and just as the cops pulled up onto the property—it was a big farmhouse with servants on a lot of acres, like something Hans Christian Andersen would put in a story—the pilot pulled back on the control stick and we took off. A couple days later, my client and his son are back to living together as a family, safe and sound in the United States.

15

Delegate.

You might think that a New York City street cop, one who never bowed to departmental rules or got along well with the command bureaucracy, would find becoming a manager distasteful. But Bo understands that an effective executive, whether at the CEO or middle-management level, must be able to delegate, to get things done through others.

But when the employees under your supervision run into obstacles in getting the job done, you as a manager may have to step in to get past the roadblocks in their way, if those obstacles are too great for the employees themselves to overcome.

At age fifty-four, Bo has reached a point in his life where he doesn't need to be in the thick of the action all the time. In fact, for

Beau Dietl & Associates, having Bo involved in difficult or controversial cases can sometimes be a PR liability.

■   ■   ■

I am an exposed person today, so if something goes wrong with a case and I am personally involved, it becomes the headline in tomorrow's newspaper.

A case in point was the Howard Beach incident, where a group of white boys was accused of chasing a young black man, causing him to run into traffic and get killed.

I was called in to investigate, and I quickly discovered that the situation was not what the mayor's office or the press had claimed.

What happened was that a bunch of drug dealers, who happened to be black, went into a mostly white neighborhood. At a local pizza parlor, there was a confrontation between the drug dealers and the neighborhood youths. Allegedly, the white kids chased one of the black kids with baseball bats, into traffic, where he was hit and killed by a car going sixty miles an hour. We proved that two of the black youths had pulled knives on the white kids first. Then, in response, the white kids had pulled out baseball bats.

I went to Howard Beach and personally interviewed numerous witnesses, including the mother of one of the black boys involved. That afternoon, the FBI called me down to their offices. They said I had told the mother that I was an FBI agent, which of course was not true. "That's ridiculous," I told the FBI. "I'm a retired NYPD homicide detective, so I don't have to make up some bullshit about being with the FBI. I still carry a duplicate of my shield, and I tell people the truth: that I am a retired NYPD homicide detective."

My investigation uncovered the truth: The youngster who ran out into the highway was high on cocaine; it wasn't being chased that made him reckless, it was drugs. He was standing on an island in the middle of the highway, and no one came after him. He ran out into the road and thought he could make it because the coke clouded his judgment.

We found out what really happened, but the FBI was almost ready to believe a story about me, which could have gotten in the way of our investigation and overshadowed the facts.

So, what would it be like to have Bo Dietl as a boss?

"If you do your job, you have my full confidence. If you do not, I will come down hard on you."

Making a mistake is okay in my book, but covering it up is not. I tell my investigators, "If you are tailing a guy and you lose him, that's okay; just tell me you screwed up. But don't make up stories."

I was so honest as a cop that it sometimes got me into trouble with my superiors, because if I don't like someone, I tell him what I think. I want my employees, clients, and business associates to do the same with me: If you have something to say, say it to my face, but don't talk about me behind my back.

Is honesty always the best policy?

Always tell the truth. When you tell the truth, you don't have to remember what you said. When you make up a story, you have to remember it, and you get lost, and you are always caught.

It's possible that telling the truth may have cost me the election when I ran for Congress in 1986, but I had to be true—both to myself and to the voters in his district.

I was a white Italian ex-cop running for Congress in a district that was fifty percent black against a black reverend. When I would go into Jamaica, Queens, to campaign, I would get booed. They said, "You're not one of us, this isn't your neighborhood, and you don't know our problems."

Instead of turning my back on these critics, I confronted them head-on. I told the crowd, "I *do* know the problems of the black community, because I worked in East Harlem as a cop. Your problem is that your community suffers from crime, half of which you don't report because you believe the cops won't do anything about it. I understand what crack is doing to your community, because when I arrested the most notorious mass murderer in New York City, he was high on crack."

The murderer, Christopher Thomas, was response for the so-called Palm Sunday Massacre, in which eight children, ages three to twelve, and two adults were each murdered by two shots in the head. As a member of the special task force investigating the crime, I investigated hundreds of leads and conducted interviews resulting in Thomas's apprehension and conviction.

8 WAYS TO IMPROVE YOUR MANAGERIAL SKILLS

As a manager, your success is measured not by your own output but by the output and productivity of the people you supervise.

Fortunately, working with others and getting them to give you their best can be just as rewarding as your individual work—once you get the hang of it. Here are eight tips that will help you manage and guide your people more effectively.

1. *Use the human touch.* Some valuable qualities that you can develop within yourself are patience, kindness, and consideration for other people. Although machines and chemicals don't care whether you scream and curse at them, people do.

Your subordinates are not just engineers, administrators, clerks, and programmers. They're *people,* first and foremost—people with families and friends, likes and dislikes, people with feelings. Respect them as people and you'll get *their* respect and loyalty in return. But treat them coldly and impersonally and they will lose motivation to perform for you.

Corny as it sounds, the Golden Rule—"Do unto others as you would have others do unto you"—is a sound, proven management principle. The next time you're about to discipline a worker or voice your displeasure, ask yourself, *Would I like to be spoken to the way I'm thinking of speaking to him or her?* Give your people the same kindness and consideration that you would want to receive if you were in their place.

2. Don't be overly critical. As a manager, it's part of your job to keep your people on the right track. And that involves pointing out errors and telling them where they've gone wrong.

But some managers are *overly* critical. They're not happy unless they are criticizing. They rarely accomplish much or take on anything new themselves, but they are only too happy to tell *others* where they went wrong, why they're doing it incorrectly, and why they could do the job better.

Don't be this type of person. Chances are, you have more knowledge and experience in your field than a good many of the people you supervise. But that's why the company made you the boss. Your job is to guide and *teach* these people, not to yell or nitpick or show them how dumb they are compared to you.

Mary Kay Ash, founder and director of Mary Kay cosmetics, says that successful managers encourage their people instead of criticizing them. "Forget their mistakes," she advises, "and zero in on one small thing they do right. Praise them, and they'll do more things right and discover talents and abilities they never realized they had."

3. Let them fail. Of course, to follow through on Mary Kay's advice, you've got to let your people make some mistakes.

Does this shock you? I'm not surprised. Most workers expect to be punished for every mistake. Most managers think it's a "black eye" on their record when an employee goofs.

But successful managers know that the best way for their people to learn and grow is through experience, and that means taking chances and making errors.

Give your people the chance to try new skills or tasks without a supervisor looking over their shoulder, but only on smaller, less crucial projects. That way, mistakes won't hurt the company and can be corrected quickly and easily. On major projects, where performance is critical, you'll want to give as much supervision as is needed to ensure successful completion of the task.

4. *Be available.* Have you ever been enthusiastic about a project, only to find yourself stuck, unable to continue, while you waited for someone higher up to check your work before giving the go-ahead for the next phase?

Few things dampen employee motivation more than management's inattention. As a manager, you have a million things to worry about besides the report that's sitting in your mailbox, waiting for your approval. But to the person who wrote that report, each day's delay causes frustration, anger, worry, and insecurity.

So, although you've got a lot to do, give your first attention to approving, reviewing, and okaying projects in progress. If employees stop by to ask questions or discuss projects, invite them to sit down for a few minutes. If you're pressed for time, set up an appointment for later that day, and keep it. This will let your people know that you are genuinely interested in them. And that's something they'll really appreciate.

5. *Improve the workplace.* People are most productive when they have the right tools and work in pleasant, comfortable surroundings. According to a study by the Buffalo Organization, a comfortable office environment creates an extra $1,600 of productivity annually for professionals and managers.

Be aware that you may not be the best judge of what your employees need to do their jobs effectively. Even if you've done the job yourself, someone else may work best with a different set of tools or in a different setup, because each person is different.

If your people complain about work conditions, *listen*. These complaints are usually not made for self-gain, but stem from each worker's desire to do the *best job possible*. And by providing the right equipment or work space, you can achieve enormous increases in output with a minimal investment.

6. *Have a personal interest in people.* When is the last time you asked your secretary how her son was doing in Little League or how she enjoyed her vacation?

Good salespeople know that relating to the customer on a person-to-person level is the fastest way to win friends and sales. Yet many technical managers remain aloof and avoid conversation that does not relate directly to business. Why? Perhaps it's because engineers are more comfortable with equations and inanimate objects than with people, and feel uncomfortable in social situations.

But just as a salesperson wants to get to know his customer, you can benefit by showing a little personal interest in your people—their problems, family life, health, and hobbies. This doesn't have to be insincere or overdone, just the type of routine conversation that should naturally pass between people who work closely.

If you've been ignoring your employees, get into the habit of taking a few minutes every week (or every day) to say hello and chat for a minute or two. If an employee has a personal problem affecting his or her mood or performance, try to find out what it is and how you might help. Send a card or small gift on important occasions and holidays, such as a tenth anniversary with the firm or a birthday. Often, it is the little things that we do for people (such as letting workers with long commutes leave early on a snowy day, or springing for dinner when overtime is required) that have the biggest effect on their loyalty to you.

7. Be open to new ideas. You might think the sign of a good manager is a department where everybody is busy at work on their assigned tasks. But if your people are merely "doing their jobs," they're only working at about half their potential. A truly productive department is one in which every employee is actively thinking of better, more efficient methods of working and ways to produce a higher quality product in less time and at a lower cost.

To get this kind of innovation from your people, you have to be receptive to new ideas; what's more, you have to encourage your people to produce new ideas. Incentives are one way you can motivate your staff. You can offer a cash bonus, time off, or a gift. But a more potent form of motivation is simply making sure the employees know that management does listen and does put employee suggestions and ideas to work. The old standby, the suggestion box, is a time-tested method of putting this into action.

And when you listen to new ideas, be open-minded. Don't shoot down a suggestion before you've heard it in full. Many of us are too quick, too eager, to show off our own experience and knowledge and say that something won't work because "we've tried it before" or "we don't do it that way." Well, maybe you did try it before, but that doesn't mean it won't work now. And having done things a certain way in the past doesn't necessarily mean you've been doing them the best way. A good manager is always receptive to new ideas.

8. *Give your people a place to grow in their careers.* If a worker doesn't have a position to aspire to or a promotion to work toward, then his or her job is a dead end. And dead-end workers are usually bored, unhappy, and unproductive. Organize your department so that everyone has the opportunity for advancement, and so that there is a logical progression up the ladder in terms of title, responsibility, status, and pay.

If this isn't possible because your department is too small, perhaps that progression must inevitably lead to jobs *outside* the department. If so, don't hold people back; instead, encourage them to aim for these goals so that they will put forth their best efforts during all the years they are with you.

16

Hire the best. Then reward those who work the hardest for you and get the best results.

Are most owners of small businesses good at hiring?

Not if you, like Bo, believe that a key to business success is hiring the best people, and then giving them the freedom and motivation to do the best job they can.

A few years ago, for example, a survey by Challenger, Gray & Christmas found that three out of five owners of small businesses were not selective about the people they hired. They simply hire whoever is available when they need to increase production output.

Unfortunately, the result is often unqualified, inept staff who affect the bottom line with poor customer service and inferior product quality.

Bo believes in hiring the best employees you can find, because whatever your business, it can give you a competitive edge.

"What has made BDA a successful company is the quality of people Dietl has handpicked to work for him," according to an article in *GQ* magazine. "Seasoned detectives he knew from the force, former FBI guys, lawyers, and especially his partner, Mike Ciravolo, who was the commanding officer of a detective squad in Queens." His staff at Beau Dietl & Associates also includes former New York City prosecutors, retired DEA agents, and organized-crime busters.

But it's more than just about hiring good people, explains Bo. What's really critical is to know the skills, talents, and assets that your organization needs to deliver a superior product or service to its customers; then find, hire, and train people who possess those attributes.

A case in point: A wealthy Greenwich, Connecticut, executive was desperate to find his fifteen-year-old daughter, who had run away from home to follow the band Phish.

■　　■　　■

I knew the easiest way to track her down was to go undercover at Phish concerts. But I am a two-hundred-pound, beat-shaped ex-cop in his fifties. I'd stand out like a sore thumb at a Phish concert; my cover would never hold.

My solution? I assigned a twenty-four-year-old associate, Sean Lanigan, to go undercover, disguised as a hippie, at a Phish concert in Las Vegas. He found the girl selling peanut butter and jelly sandwiches from the back of a Volkswagen van. By nightfall, her father was on board his private jet, on his way to pick her up.

"You send in a retired police officer in his forties or fifties, he looks suspicious," says Sean. "When you see me, your first impression is, 'This guy's not a cop.'"

In another case, Sean went undercover as a janitor in a nursing home in an attempt to catch employees sabotaging the facility before going on strike. He also once caught a seventy-eight-year-old woman being unfaithful to her eighty-year-old husband. He even tailed a rabbi recovering from sex addiction to make sure he had not reverted to his old ways (he had not).

Many of the retired police officers who work for Beau Dietl & Associates are older guys who went to school and completed their careers in the pre-Internet era. While they know how to interview a suspect or examine a crime scene, they aren't comfortable with doing research online, which has become an essential element in the private investigations industry.

That's why even though I have a reputation for hiring mainly ex-cops as my investigators, I now have a number of employees in their twenties who sit in a row of cubicles, clicking away at computer terminals and checking résumés of potential hires of Fortune 500 client companies to see, for example, if the candidates really graduated from the schools they list. They are supervised by Frank Renaud, who has a Ph.D. in economics.

Jennifer, age twenty-four, has found in her computer searches that executives at prominent companies lied about their college educations. She is also good at "pretext calls"—calling people under false pretenses to get information from them.

Steve, twenty-seven, is a graduate of the American Musical and Dramatic Academy. "I don't have a gun and never jump on cars," says Steve. "The only weapons we have are laptops."

The one problem with hiring younger investigators is that they are getting the idea from TV that this life is more glamorous than it really is. I'm pretty careful to give new recruits a reality check before I hire them about what they can expect when working for BDA. The majority of it is tedious work. Even surveillance can be boring; you're out there for twelve hours, looking at a freakin' door.

Although I'm known as a hard guy, I'm soft when it comes to letting my people go.

The rule is that you should hire slow and fire fast. If an employee is a nonperformer and can't get his act together, you harm your company and your relationships with your clients, and you are even doing the underperforming employee a disservice by keeping him on.

Unfortunately, for me, this is one of those areas in which I am anything but tough. I hate to fire people, and I will do whatever I can to avoid it—even though I know it's what I should do. I feel sorry for people, and it's difficult for me to cut them loose.

For instance, a year or so ago, I brought on board a CEO who promised me that he was a "rainmaker"—an executive able to bring lots of new business to Beau Dietl & Associates.

He had been the head of security for a large insurance company whose business we wanted to get. The contract was worth $6 million, and he assured me that he could bring it with him.

But the new client didn't materialize—and neither did any other new business—from this so-called rainmaker.

I called him into my office and asked him how much new business he had brought us since I made him CEO. He answered by asking me how much new business I had brought in lately. I told him, "You should resign and go teach criminal justice in a college or something." He resigned, saving me from having to fire him.

My employees earn salaries far higher than the industry average. I pay more in every avenue of service than any other company in our business. In return, I expect the people I hire to be worth it.

I recently hired a new president. I told him, "You can go as far in this company as you want to go. I am holding out the baton to you. All you have to do is take it."

So far, I like what I see. We were preparing a major proposal to provide security for a county in Pennsylvania, and this guy called me at home Sunday to ask some questions about it—from the office. That's dedication. He was showing me that he was in the game and that he takes it seriously.

I told my new executive, "You can be the CEO, you can be the president, you can be anything you want. I will give a title to anyone who earns it, but you have to work to hold on to it."

However, hiring additional staff is not always the best strategy for adding new talent to your business. In some cases, it makes more sense to outsource work to subcontractors or to form alliances with professionals offering services that are complementary to your own.

For instance, although BDA is not a law firm, many of the activities we investigate are criminal, and so it makes sense for us to offer our clients access to legal expertise.

Rather than hire a new attorney out of law school, I put my network of contacts to work again, and BDA recently announced that it was partnering with world-renowned attorney James J.

Binns, a trial lawyer who specializes in white-collar criminal cases.

Binns is an expert in his field but also a colorful character, both of which make him a good fit for partnering with me. Licensed to practice law in twenty states, Binns is a member of the bar of the United States Supreme Court. A member of the Pennsylvania Boxing Hall of Fame, Binns played the part of Rocky Balboa's lawyer in the motion picture *Rocky V.*

Another world-renowned attorney, the personal injury lawyer John Quinlan Kelly, is also part of my team. Kelly worked the civil case against O.J. Simpson, as well as many other high-profile cases.

17

Find a need and fill it.

One of the truisms about business so commonly known that it borders on cliché is: Find a need and fill it.

The process is simple: Identify a pressing need in the market—preferably one that is serious and urgent, and one that your customers want to take care of right away. Then be the first to innovate a product or service to fill that need.

For instance, in the wake of 9/11, corporations began to worry about anthrax-contaminated mail in their mail rooms.

On December 10, 2001, Beau Dietl & Associates announced the launch of a new wholly owned subsidiary, BDA Mail Screening Services, designed to deal with the anthrax threat.

Working out of a warehouse in the Hell's Kitchen section of Manhattan, BDA Mail Screening Services employs about two dozen people to screen client mail. To ensure worker safety, the employees wear hazardous-materials suits.

They use a mail-screening technology certified by the federal government to sterilize mail. Workers cover their eyes with goggles to protect them from the radiation of the blue lamps that cleanse the mail for anthrax.

No one knows when the next wave of contamination will happen. What we are selling is peace of mind.

I've made profits by identifying problems clients have and then offering them new solutions.

For instance, I noticed that a common problem in business is the time it takes to be cleared at a company's reception desk. You'll be running late for a meeting, standing in line at the reception desk, waiting to be cleared for entry, and held up by people in the reception area who are uncaring, rude, or indifferent.

In response, BDA introduced a "Reception Staff Service." Clients can outsource the staffing of the reception area to Beau Dietl & Associates, eliminating the need to recruit, train, and have such staff on their own payroll.

To ensure that visitors receive a courteous reception, BDA Reception Staff Service personnel receive extensive training in Concierge Serving by one of the most renown leaders in this field. They also receive in-depth training in the nuances of security work, ensuring the safety of a company's facilities and personnel.

And when the new U.S. Patriot Act permitted companies to be fined up to one million dollars for failing to verify the true identity of their investors, maintain records containing information about those investors, or consulting the U.S. Treasury Department regarding their most current listing of suspected terrorists, we added another new offering to the list of services provided by Beau Dietl & Associates—the "U.S. Patriot Act Compliance."

We screen customers on either a national or international level. We will ascertain any relevant criminal records, profile pertinent business relationships, determine sources of assets, and outline negative litigation histories. Our process ensures that our clients are not unwittingly being used to launder illicit money or fund terrorist activities.

A TECHNIQUE FOR PRODUCING BUSINESS IDEAS

Let's say you want to find a need and fill it. How do you get ideas for products or services? Here is what you should do: Identify the problem, assemble pertinent facts, gather general knowledge, look for combinations, sleep on it, use a checklist, get feedback, team up, and give new ideas a chance.

1. Identify the problem. The first step in solving a problem is to know what the problem is. But many of us forge ahead without knowing what it is we are trying to accomplish. Moral: Don't apply a solution before you have taken the time to accurately define the problem.

2. Assemble pertinent facts. In crime stories, detectives spend most of their time looking for clues. They cannot solve a case with clever thinking alone; they must have the facts. You, too, must have the facts before you can solve a problem or make an informed decision.

Professionals in every field know the importance of gathering specific facts. A scientist planning an experiment checks the abstracts to see what similar experiments have been performed. An author writing a book collects everything he or she can on the subject—newspaper clippings, photos, official records, transcripts of interviews, diaries, magazine articles, and so on. A consultant may spend weeks or months digging around a company before coming up with a solution to a major problem.

Keep an organized file of the background material that you collect on a project. Review the file before you begin to formulate your solution. If you are a competent typist, use a typewriter or word processor to rewrite your research notes and materials. This step increases your familiarity with the background information and can give you a fresh perspective on the problem. Also, when you type notes, you condense a mound of material into a few neat pages that show all the facts at a glance.

3. Gather general knowledge. "Specific facts" have to do with the project at hand. They include the budget, the schedule, the resources available, and the customer's specifications, plus knowledge of the products, components, and techniques to be used in completing the project.

General knowledge has to do with the expertise you've developed in business, and includes your storehouse of information concerning life, events, people, science, technology, management, and the world at large.

In most plants, it is the gray-haired foreman, the twenty-year veteran, who the young workers turn to when they have problems. This senior worker is able to solve so many problems so quickly not because he is brighter or better educated than others, but because in his twenty years of plant work, he has seen those problems—or similar ones—before.

You can't match the senior man's experience. But you can accelerate your own education by becoming a student in the many areas that relate to your job. Trade journals are the most valuable source of general business knowledge. Subscribe to the journals that relate to your field. Scan them all, and clip and save articles that contain information that may be useful to you. Organize your clippings in files for easy access to articles by subject.

Read books in your field and start a reference library. Think back to that twenty-year plant foreman. If he writes a book on how to troubleshoot problems in a chemical plant, and you buy the book, you can learn in a day or so of reading what it took him twenty years to accumulate. Take some night-school courses. Attend seminars, conferences, and trade shows. Make friends with people in your field and exchange information, stories, ideas, case histories, and technical tips.

Most of the successful professionals I know are compulsive information-collectors. You should be, too.

4. Look for new combinations. Someone once complained to me, "There's nothing new in the world. It's all been done before." Maybe. But an idea doesn't have to be something completely new. Many ideas are simply new combinations of existing elements. By looking for combinations, for new relationships between old ideas, you can come up with a fresh approach.

The clock radio, for example, was invented by someone who combined two existing technologies: the clock and the radio.

Look for synergistic combinations when you examine the facts. What two things can work together to form a third thing? That is a new idea. If you have two devices, and each performs a function you need, can you link them together to create a new invention?

5. Sleep on it. Putting the problem aside for a time can help you renew your idea-producing powers just when you think your creative well has run dry.

But don't resort to this method after only five minutes of puzzled thought. First, you have to gather all the information you can. Next, you need to go over the information again and again as you try to come up with that one big idea. You'll come to a point where you get bleary, punch-drunk, just hashing the same ideas over and over. This is the time to take a break, to put the problem aside, to sleep on it, and to let your unconscious mind take over.

A solution may strike you as you sleep, shower, shave, or walk in the park. Even if it doesn't, when you return to the problem, you will find that you can attack it with renewed vigor and a fresh perspective. Many times, the things that I thought were brilliant when I wrote them can be much improved at a second glance.

6. Use a checklist. Checklists can be used to stimulate creative thinking and as a starting point for new ideas. Many manufacturers, consultants, technical magazines, and trade associations publish checklists that you can use in your own work. But the best checklists are those that you create yourself, because they are tailored to the problems that come up in your daily routine.

For example, Jill is a technical salesperson who is well versed in the features of her product, but she has trouble when it comes to closing a sale. She could overcome this weakness by making a checklist of typical customer objections and how to answer them. (This list of objections can be culled from sales calls made over the course of several weeks. Possible tactics for overcoming these objections can be garnered from fellow salespeople, from books on selling, and from her own trial-and-error efforts.) Then, when faced with a tough customer, she won't have to reinvent the wheel—instead, she will be prepared for all the standard objections, because she is familiar with the checklist.

However, no checklist can contain an idea for every situation that could come up. Remember, a checklist should be used as a tool for creative thinking, not as a crutch.

7. Get feedback. Getting someone else's opinion of your

work can help you focus your thinking and produce ideas you hadn't thought of.

Take the feedback for what it's worth. If you feel you are right, and the criticisms are off base, ignore them. But more often than not, feedback will provide useful information that can help you come up with the best, most profitable ideas.

Of course, if you ask others to take a look at your report, you should be willing to do the same for them when they solicit your opinion. You'll find that reviewing the work of others is fun; it's easier to critique someone else's work than to find mistakes in your own. And you'll be gratified by the improvements you think of—things that are obvious to you but would never have occurred to the other person.

8. Team up. Some people think more creatively when they are working in groups. But how large should the group be? My opinion is that two people are the ideal team. Any more and you're in danger of ending up with a committee that spins its wheels and accomplishes nothing. The person you team up with should have skills and thought processes that balance and complement your own. For example, in advertising, copywriters (the word people) team up with art directors (the picture people).

In entrepreneurial firms, the idea person who started the company will often hire a professional manager from one of the Fortune 500 companies as the new venture grows; the entrepreneur knows how to make things happen, but the manager knows how to run a profitable, efficient corporation.

If you are an engineer, you may invent a better microchip. But if you want to make a fortune selling it, you should team up with someone who has a strong sales and marketing background.

9. *Give new ideas a chance.* Many businesspeople, especially managerial types, develop their critical faculties more finely than their creative faculties. If creative engineers and inventors had listened to these people, we would not have personal computers, cars, airplanes, lightbulbs, or electricity.

The creative process works in two stages. The first is the idea-producing stage, when ideas flow freely. The second is the critical or editing stage, when you hold each idea up to the cold light of day and see if it is practical.

Many of us make the mistake of mixing the stages together. During the idea-producing stage, we are too eager to criticize an idea as soon as it is presented. As a result, we shoot down ideas and make snap judgments when we should be encouraging the production of ideas. And many good ideas are killed this way.

18

Do the right thing.

"Bo Dietl is ruddered by an imperturbable belief that he knows the difference between right and wrong and that he can change the world to make it a better place."
—GREG GUSS, *EGO* MAGAZINE

I will not sacrifice my principles for money—even if it means a loss of millions of dollars in potential revenue for one of my companies.

For instance, the War in Iraq has become a large, lucrative business for many U.S. corporations. Vice President Dick Cheney's former company, Halliburton, took in $3.6 billion in 2003 from contracts to serve U.S. troops and rebuild the oil industry in Iraq. Also, Fluor Corporation's joint venture with

AMEC has $1.7 billion in contracts to rebuild Iraq's electricity, water, sewer, and waste-removal infrastructure. And Northrop Grumman's Vinnell Corp. subsidiary was awarded a $48 million contract to train the new Iraqi army. The U.S. Army estimates that between 124,000 and 605,000 Americans are working as private contractors in Iraq.

Security—the primary source of revenue for Beau Dietl & Associates—is also a big business in Iraq.

According to a CNN report, more than four thousand private-sector security personnel are working in Iraq at rates ranging from $350 to $1,500 per day.

But I said no to any and all offers for BDA to provide security services in Iraq. The reason is simple: I don't want to put my employees in unnecessary danger. I could not live with myself if even one BDA employee working security in Iraq was killed. I would feel totally responsible to that person's family, and depriving them of a father, husband, or son is a risk I am not willing to take.

Other companies seem more than willing to put their employees in danger when profits are at stake: At least fifty-five Halliburton employees and subcontractors have been killed in Iraq and Kuwait. But my employees will never be sent into a war zone.

If you are not firmly convinced that there is an ethics crisis in corporate America today, think back on these famous names: Adelphia, Enron, Arthur Andersen, Xerox, WorldCom, Tyco, ImClone, Martha Stewart.

Corruption is nothing new to me. I grew up in a Queens neighborhood where mobsters were both neighbors and friends.

Later, I joined the police force, where for some, being on the take is a way of life.

The situation seems not to be much different in America's corporate boardrooms. But why is there so much corruption at every level of business and government today?

It's simple: People are greedy, and the temptation to go for the quick buck is, for many, too great to resist.

According to a study by the Ethics Officer Association, 48 percent of surveyed employees admitted to illegal or unethical actions, and half said they used technology unethically on the job during the year.

In a poll by the American Society of Chartered Life Underwriters, 57 percent of workers felt more pressured now than five years ago to consider acting unethically or illegally on the job. Forty percent said the pressure has increased over the last twelve months. In response, more than five hundred ethics courses are now offered today at American business schools.

I don't need to take an ethics course, but I certainly could teach one.

For my entire adult life, I have been obsessed with doing the right thing, simply because it is the right thing to do, and not because of the potential reward.

A few years ago, Beau Dietl & Associates bid on a $34 million contract to provide security for the World Trade Center. Getting the business would have been by far BDA's biggest business win and would have added million of dollars to BDA's bottom line. But after I questioned stipulated union benefits, my originally accepted bid was awarded to another security company.

I protected the citizen witnesses in my cases from threats and violence before and during trials; you think I'm not going to protect my own employees? I used to show up at work with abused or abandoned kids who I found during my investigations.

Under the department rules, you are supposed to bring endangered children into the precinct and notify the Bureau of Child Welfare, but almost no one did it. There's an unwritten code in the department that says you don't get involved—a code that I routinely ignored.

After leaving the NYPD, one day while I was relaxing at home I looked out my window and saw someone I didn't know in front of my neighbor's house, trying to open the front door unsuccessfully. The guy then walked to the next house and began pulling at that door.

Still in my bathrobe, I ran out the front door and across the street to my neighbor's front yard, where I grabbed the guy and took away a knife that he was carrying. I stopped a robbery, and the guy, wanted in several burglary cases, was arrested.

Important too, I didn't use more force than what was needed. I've always preferred my fists to guns. Even when someone I was arresting shot at me five times, I didn't shoot him. But I did shatter his jaw when I punched him in the face. My knuckles and the backs of my hands have tiny white scars from years of hand-to-hand street combat.

And while I never thought I used excessive force, I certainly was not above the threat of violence—if it meant getting the job done.

Once, I threatened to burn down a suspect's house unless the man let me in to conduct a search—the guy had just killed five people, so I wasn't feeling too patient.

But when the violence is unjustified, even if it involved the cops vs. a suspect, I cannot condone it.

Look at the Abner Louima case, where a Haitian immigrant was allegedly assaulted and sodomized with a plunger by New York City cops.

Maybe Louima resisted, and if a suspect is violent, sometimes you have to fight back hard enough to put him down. But this? Forget it! The defense attorney for some of the cops involved asked me to do some detective work on their case, but I turned him down. I am nauseated by what they did, and the damage it does to the reputation of the police force.

Although I carry a gun today and did so as a member of the NYPD for sixteen years, I only fired my gun once in the line of duty—and that was over a suspect's head, just to scare him and get him to stop resisting arrest.

In fact, when Congresswoman Carolyn McCarthy, whose husband and son were victims of the Long Island Railroad Massacre, began lobbying for stricter gun control in New York, I came out to support her.

I am one hundred percent against assault weapons because all I see is them being used against cops. People think of me as my *One Tough Cop* persona, a tough guy, a fighter. But that is not the way I feel on this issue.

19

Believe in yourself.

When it comes to achieving success, nothing can hold you back more than lack of self-confidence.

Conversely, few things can lead to long-term success than reliance: being strong enough to bounce back and go on in the face of enormous adversity.

For example, at the height of the dot-com era, I was involved in a technology venture with my partner Danny DelGiorno. We sold the company for a lot of money; we had about $50 million in our control. You gotta understand, I grew up a poor kid in Queens, and I never in my life could imagine having so much money.

So we invested most of it into a bunch of other technology companies, which we were certain would take us from millions to a billion. But then the dot-com bubble burst, and most of those companies went down the toilet.

Flush with money, I also got caught up in the bull market and tech-stock boom.

I would be eating dinner at my usual table at Rao's with my buddies, and some guy would start talking about a hot stock. What did I know? They all sounded good to me, and I had a lot of money. "Bo, this is a great company, and it's only a dollar a share," a guy would tell me. So I'd call a broker and say, "Buy me two hundred thousand shares."

The only problem was that the market went crazy, and these were shit stocks you couldn't sell. Between my high-tech stocks and my high-tech companies, my losses were in the millions of dollars.

More recently, we suffered a setback at Beau Dietl & Associates, where an inept CEO cost the company millions in lost revenues. But we're coming back. Billings are on the rise again, thanks in part to heightened post-9/11 security concerns, and thanks to my own efforts, along with those of my new president.

As for investments, Steve Witkoff and I own millions of dollars in Manhattan real estate. We're also in some real estate development deals that are quite lucrative. And we bought several brands from Unilever that are making us a lot of money.

The key is, I'm always looking for the next big deal, the next business opportunity. At the moment, I'm excited about my latest venture, a nutritional-supplement company that sells fish oil.

Maybe it's because I never had money for most of my life, but

I'm not afraid of failure or being poor. Failure is a temporary condition, and it is often a necessary one to experience on the road to success.

Thomas Edison tried and failed a thousand times to make a lightbulb. But on experiment number 1,001, it worked. And I think he did okay. (For the record, Edison applied for and was granted a total of 1,093 patents.)

There's never a job in front of me that I think I can't get done. When I was a detective, the guys nicknamed me "the pit bull."

I am relentless. If I feel someone was wronged, I will go above and beyond the call of duty to get to the truth.

I remember working the anticrime unit in East Harlem. A gang was terrorizing the neighborhood, shaking down Hispanic store owners and raping young girls.

I had to dismantle this gang, and I would not back off. My strategy: Find out which members of the gang were its officers and go after them one at a time. I went after each one individually; I had fistfights with each one, and I would not stop until I had locked all of them up.

The gang president was wanted on suspicion of raping a twelve-year-old girl, but I needed to catch him in the act of committing a crime. Then came my big break.

I saw a bunch of the gang members walking down Lexington Avenue, all wearing kelly-green tuxedos. When I asked them what they were doing, they said they were going to the wedding of the gang president, which was being held on 117th Street.

I knew he was addicted to cocaine, so I went to the wedding

hall on 117th Street and waited outside. Sure enough, he came out of the hall to sniff some coke. When he did, I grabbed him, threw him against my car, and arrested him.

He and all the gang members complained about me arresting him on his wedding day; 150 of the gang members stormed the station house to protest. But he didn't give that twelve-year-old girl a chance to protest when he raped her, so I didn't think he deserved one, either.

20

Think big.

"Who knows what it is about New York—the palpable energy, the vertiginous architecture, the PCB levels in the water supply—that makes it such a fertile ground for men with thunderous egos: Giuliani, Steinbrenner, Trump, Sharpton, Dietl," writes Lucky Kaylin in *GQ*. "Bo might not be as well known as these guys, but in terms of a desire to big-foot his way into legend, he is their equal."

When Bo retired from the NYPD, he—like many other law-enforcement officers—decided to go into the job he knew so well, security, as a private investigator.

Overwhelmingly, the majority of private investigators are small one- or two-man agencies run out of a home or apartment, or the stereotypical dingy little office in a walk-up building. Bo, too, started his PI practice working out of his home in Queens.

Right from the start, he was successful—or, at least, other people looking at him objectively would say that he was successful.

One of his first clients was the famous attorney Myron Beldock, who called Bo because he had read the article about him in *New York* magazine.

Beldock was representing Darryl King, who has been behind bars seventeen years for killing a cop. "No way I'm going to help a cop killer," said Bo. But Beldock explained that King was innocent, and he wanted Bo's help to prove it. Bo agreed but told the attorney, "What I investigate is the truth. Whether the truth hurts you or not, you asked for it and that is what you get. If I find this guy really killed the cop, I would pull the switch on the electric chair myself."

But Bo found that Beldock was right: King was innocent. "An Agent for ATF [the Bureau of Alcohol, Tobacco, Firearms, and Explosives] who had worked the case told me that two other men killed the cop. The cop had fired back, and when King was arrested, they were in a hospital." (The two killers are dead from other causes.) Bo took the evidence to Beldock, and King was released from jail about eight years ago.

"I believe in justice for all people," says Bo. "If you have been wronged, I want you to get equal justice, and I will be relentless in getting it for you."

Bo's annual earnings the year he retired from the force—base salary plus overtime—were $40,000. In his first full year in business as a private investigator, Bo's one-man practice earned $220,000—more than five times what he made on the force. And this was back in 1985, when six figures meant more than it does today.

But Bo wasn't content to do things in a small way. He built his business from a solo PI to one of the largest security companies in the country, shifting away from divorce cases and other typical PI fare to the bigger and more lucrative arena of corporate security for Fortune 500 clients.

Within twelve years after getting his PI license, Bo had built BDA to annual revenues in excess of $10 million. More than 70 percent of the company's revenues are generated by white-collar-crime investigations for corporate clients.

In the process, BDA moved from modest offices in Queens to large, luxurious offices in midtown Manhattan. Not only does Beau Dietl & Associates have its headquarters on the thirty-fifth and twenty-fifth floors of the prestigious Daily News building (where the motion picture *Superman* was filmed), Bo and his real estate partner, Steve Witkoff, once owned the entire building, which they later sold.

From his office window, Bo was able to see the twin towers of the World Trade Center before they fell on 9/11. His office is lined with mahogany bookshelves. In the bookcases and on the walls are trophies, plaques, awards, bric-a-brac, and police certificates of honor.

There are photos of Bo with politicians and celebrities: Yogi Berra, Senator Al D'Amato, Michael Jackson (for whom Bo has done security work), Ronald Reagan, and George W. Bush. There's also a framed thank-you note from General Norman

Schwarzkopf for his autographed copy of Bo's book, and several framed articles mentioning Bo.

On the coffee table are binoculars for glancing at attractive women sunbathers on nearby roofs during the summer months, and a giant stuffed owl wearing the Ellis Island Medal of Honor. Under the glass tabletop are passes to the Republican National Convention and the Grammy Awards.

Many of us would be exhausted living Bo's life for just one week—or even for one day. He has a huge appetite for life, whether it's making million-dollar deals, hobnobbing with the rich and famous and powerful, or sitting down to a power dinner with his colleagues, clients, and friends.

Legendary trenchermen like A. J. Liebling and "Diamond Jim" Brady often ate meals that defied description. Brady was found by doctors to have stretched his stomach to six times its normal size.

Unlike Liebling and Brady, Bo remains fit and healthy. But his gusto for life also carries over to the table.

Bo often takes a Zantac in preparation for what one reporter described as his "power feasting" at which "platters of shrimp, pasta, stuffed clams, and pork chops come swooping down like saucers from planet Pig-out, followed by cheesecake, port, and espresso."

At these power dinners, the meal is "accompanied by aggressive repartee, punctuated by the aggressive bleat of cell phones and regular rounds of machine-gun guffaws, all in response to the sort of humor that veers from locker room to gutter toilet." Bo is fond of profanity and freely uses it around others in social and business situations.

In chapter 3, we talked about Bo's belief in type A and type B personalities, how he is a type A, but how even a type B can achieve major goals by following the success principles Bo has outlined here.

An article on www.hiresuccess.com says of type A personalities:

> They are the ones that are always "looking for a better way" or building a "better mousetrap." They have an entrepreneurial streak and don't mind taking risk in order to receive the rewards that can go along with it.
>
> They enjoy a challenge, and one of their biggest fears is falling into a routine. They are very decisive and persistent in getting what they want.

One of the major differences between aggressive type A and passive type B personalities is that type A's have the tendency to think big—to have grand ambitions and great dreams, and to live life to the fullest.

That's Bo to the hilt. He wears the best clothes, smokes the best cigars, drives the best cars, and dines at the best places. He doesn't like to do things in a small way. He has big ambitions. He reaches for the stars. He has money, power, and fame.

You have to ask yourself if you are that driven, if your ambitions are equally big. There's nothing wrong with having smaller dreams. But be prepared. If your ambitions are modest, your success will be, too.

There's nothing wrong with that, for some people. If that's what works for you, Bo would be the first to say great, go for it.

But if you look at the most successful people, most of them dream big and achieve big. Donald Trump's mansion is one of the largest and most expensive homes in the world; his New York City apartment is the most expensive apartment in Manhattan.

For his seventieth birthday, Malcolm Forbes threw himself a birthday party—in Morocco—that cost $2 million. He had nearly one thousand guests—mostly top names in business, entertainment, media, and the arts. The guests feasted on pigeon pie, lamb mechoui, and chicken tadjine while watching seaside fireworks. King Hassan II provided two hundred horsemen in Moroccan costume and 750 folk performers.

How big are your dreams? How successful do you want to be? Are you content to own a small, local dry-cleaning business, or do you want to own the largest chain of dry-cleaning stores in your state?

Your success will be in proportion to your visions, your dreams, and the scope of your ambitions. Bo warns against being too complacent and setting the bar too low.

There's an old story about two friends, Sam and George, who are salesmen for the same company.

They agree at the beginning of the year to write on a piece of paper their sales commission goals: how much money they want to earn that year.

At the end of the year, they get together, and George has a broad grin on his face. "I achieved my sales goal," he says proudly, pulling out his slip of paper and showing it to Sam. The figure written on it: $50,000.

"I didn't," says Sam. "I only achieved half my goal." He then shows George his slip of paper, on which he had written $500,000.

Whatever you choose—a goal of $50,000, or ten times that amount, or a hundred times that amount—Bo and I wish you well.

Until one is committed there is hesitancy, the chance to draw back, always ineffectiveness. Concerning all acts of initiative (and creation), there is one elementary truth, the ignorance of which kills countless ideas and splendid plans: that the moment one definitely commits oneself, then providence moves too.

All sorts of things occur to help one that would otherwise never have occurred. A whole stream of events issues from the decision, raising in one's favor all manner of unforeseen incidents and meetings and material assistance, which no man could have dreamt would have come his way. I have learned a deep respect for one of Goethe's couplets: "Whatever you can do, or dream you can, begin it. Boldness has genius, power, and magic in it."

—W. H. Murray

Above: Bo receiving a hero award at City Hall from Mayor Ed Koch for his involvement in what Koch labeled "The most vicious crime in New York City history," the rape and mutilation of a nun.

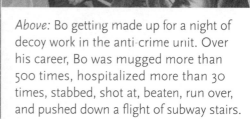

Above: Bo getting made up for a night of decoy work in the anti-crime unit. Over his career, Bo was mugged more than 500 times, hospitalized more than 30 times, stabbed, shot at, beaten, run over, and pushed down a flight of subway stairs.

Left: Police Commissioner Benjamin Ward conducts a news conference following the arrest of a suspect in the Palm Sunday massacre case.

Bo with Fleet Admiral Bob Natter (*second from left*) and friends.

(*Front*) Joel Hollander, Bo, Joseph Abboud, and Senator John McCain

Mike "The Russian," Paul Anka, Joe
Grano, Bo, and Mark Arzoomanian

Above: Bo and Don Imus

Left: Bo and Senator Bob Kerry

In the Oval Office with President Ronald Reagan

Bo with New York City Mayor Rudy Giuliani (*left*), and President Bill Clinton (*below*)

Bo and President George W. Bush (*left*) and with New York's Mayor Michael Bloomberg (*below*)

Sitting with President George H. W. Bush in the Green Room of the White House

A couple of champs:
Bo with Muhammad
Ali (*right*) and with
Andre Agassi (**below**)

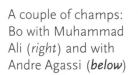

Sitting around the table
with friends (*left to right*) Dr.
Arthur Miller, Yogi Berra,
and Mel Weiss

Above: Eighteen holes with Donald Trump, Steve Witkoff, and Matt Abel

Right: The most stylish way to steer clear of the sand traps: Bo and business partner Steve Witkoff

John Myers, David Myers, Bo, and Joey "Pots and Pans"

Vinny Rao, Frank Peligno, and Bo, outside Rao's

The table at Rao's: (*back*) Joe Askin, Steve Witkoff, Sheldon Brody,
Mike "The Russian," Pete Dove; (*front*) Joseph Abboud,
Joey "Pots and Pans," Bo, and John Myers

"Bo's Way" by Paul Anka

Written and sung by Paul Anka on December 8, 2000, in honor of Bo Dietl at his 50th-birthday party

(To the tune of "Yesterday When I Was Young")

Yesterday, when you were young
With dreams yet to be dreamed
With songs yet to be sung
Life's journey was unfolding
The ride would take you high
To Mom and Dad so proudly
The apple of their eye.

Days would pass, the world would know
Right from your first communion
They'd all say, "That's our Bo!"

Outstanding in gymnastics
And soon you'd graduate
The race was just beginning
And you were at the gate.

(Into Bridge—to the tune of "My Way")

Exploring life, and then one year
You heard your calling loud and clear
As eager young police recruit
How you'd excel at each pursuit
Your life on course
First in the force
You served us your way!

(Into: to the tune of "My Way," from the top)

We send to you, dear friend, a hearty blend
Of birthday wishing
You star, have a cigar, buy a new car,
Kick back, go fishing
We say, enjoy your day; do it your way
There's fun worth tapping
The music shifts, your greatest gifts
Are friends worth "rapping"!

(Into Rep Tempo)

Like Mike "The Russian," with pals you're blessed
With Joey "Pots and Pans" and Nicky "Vest"

There's Danny and Charlie. We're glad they came
And Petey No Neck"—a common name
With Frankie Nose" any party will jump,
That achievin' Steven Witkoff who's the next Donald Trump
There's Sheldon The Tailor" and Frankie No"
And everyone at Rao's, they all love you, bro!

(Back to "My Way")

We see, devotedly, your family
For you they rally
You rank with Carol, Al, and Frank, humbly we thank
Your sweet mom, Sally
"The Fab 4" whom you adore, you can be sure
It's not the Beatles
Jaclyn, Richard, Dana, Bo
We've watched them grow
Your darling Dietls,

Out river rafting with the guys,
Gambling or leaping through the skies
Sex is like golf, we can derive
It seems you have the longest drive
What the hell, you do them well
('cause) you do them your way!

World 'round business is sound because they've found
"Dietl inspection"

You bet, our kids are set, on the Internet
With your protection
Great fate, in real estate, business is great
With Witkoff and you, sir
(And) this can't be missed, add to that list
Author and producer!

For those in need, giving's your art
You're "one tough cop" with one soft heart
So each one here is feeling blessed
To call you "friend," 'cause you're the best!
From one and all, and yours truly, Paul
Bo, happy birthday!

"Bo-isms": A Glossary

DISAFECTATED: loss of loyalty, friendship, or affection.

DOCUMENTATED: documented, proven.

IMPERFECTATIONS: problems, errors.

IMPRESSATATE: to impress someone.

LUNCHATATIONS: lunch.

OCCURATATED: took place.

PICKATATIOUS: caring, selective, particular.

PUKATATIOUS: disgusting, in poor taste, inappropriate.

REGURGITATIONS: repetition.

RETARDATATION: stupidity.

SHMUCKATATIONS: shmucks, losers.

SNAGATIOUS: a problem.

STRUCTURATATION: the structure of a situation, what happened.

TUMULTATATIOUS: tumultuous.

Appendix

Bo Dietl's Celebrity Clients (a partial list)

Babyface

Stephen Baldwin

Michael Bolton

Jon Bon Jovi

Cousin Brucie

Patrick Buchanan

Mariah Carey

David Chavez

Pat Cooper

Heavy D

Vic Damone

Robert DeNiro

Joe DiMaggio

Placido Domingo

Robert Duran

Bob Dylan

Jane Fonda

Harrison Ford

Hugh Grant

Charlton Heston

Gregory Hines

Evander Holyfield

Elizabeth Hurley

Don Imus

Amy Irving

Janet Jackson

Michael Jackson

Billy Joel

James Earl Jones

John Leguizamo

Jerry Lewis

Penelope Ann Miller

Demi Moore

Melba Moore

Tommy Mottola

Stan Musial

Al Pacino

Floyd Patterson

Sean Penn

Brad Pitt

Richard Pryor

Anthony Quinn

Trent Reznor

Diana Ross

Steven Segal

Brooke Shields

Paul Simon

Howard Stern

Ted Turner

Shania Twain

Mike Tyson

Stevie Wonder

Burt Young

Bo Dietl: Honors and Awards (a Partial List)

Governor's Award of New York State from Governor Hugh
   Carey

New York City Council Award

New York City Police Department Honor Legion Merit Award

Detectives' Crime Clinic Award of New York, New Jersey, and
   Connecticut

New York City PBA Award (Finest of the Month)

New York Daily News Award

New York City Community Council Inc. Award

Subject of *Daily News* editorial, commended as arresting officer
   (October 27, 1981)

Honor Legion Award of Merit

Detective Crime Clinic Award of New York, New Jersey, and
    Connecticut

New York's Finest Foundation Award

Award from National Puerto Rican Forum

Ellis Island Medal of Honor Award

15 Commendations of Bravery

32 Meritorious Service Awards for Bravery

15 Excellent Police Duty Awards

Bo's Political Experience

Appointed by New York Governor George E. Pataki as
    Chairman of New York State Security Advisory Committee

Member of Senator Maltese's 1999 Crime Victims & Crime
    Prevention Advisory Committee

Director of Security for New York State Republican Convention

Director of Security, National Republican Convention, Houston,
    Texas

Cochairman of National Crime Commission Appointed by
    President George Bush

Special Advisor of Law Enforcement Advisory Committee for
    1989 Inaugural Celebration

Nominated by the Republic and Conservative Parties for U.S.
    Congress for the 6th Congressional District

Special Events for Which Beau Dietl & Associates Has Handled Security

1998   Movie premiere of *Godzilla* at New York City's Madison Square Garden

1998   New York State Republican Convention

1997   Grammy Awards at Madison Square Garden

1998   Grammy Awards at Madison Square Garden

1996   New York Fund-raising Campaign for Senator Bob Dole

1995   Papal visit to Central Park, New York City

1994   New York State Republican Convention

1994   Gubernatorial Campaign for New York Governor George E. Pataki

1992   National Republican Convention in Houston, Texas

1992   Grammy Awards at Radio City Music Hall

1989   Special Advisor of the Law Enforcement Advisory Committee for the American Bi-Centennial Presidential Inaugural Celebration
        Annual Congress of Racial Equality Martin Luther King Celebrity Host Dinner
        Paul Simon & Billy Joel—Back on the Ranch Concert in Montauk, New York

BDA Company Profile

Founded in 1985, Beau Dietl & Associates (BDA) has grown to become one of the nation's most significant security and investigative firms. BDA offers a wide variety of specialized services to both corporate and individual clients. The CEO and the president of BDA, both highly decorated detectives, are retired from the New York City Police Department and maintain an excellent rapport with NYPD officials. BDA also maintains relationships with colleagues both nationally and internationally.

BDA's divisions (Corporate Services, Computer Network Security and Investigations, Special Investigations, and Security Services) offer a complete range of investigative and security services to its business and individual clients worldwide. The services range from corporate and due-diligence investigations—where information is critical to the decision-making process—to litigation support for class-action suits and civil/criminal proceedings, to providing armed security personnel, whether at home or traveling.

Moreover, BDA was designated as an Independent Private Sector Inspector General (IPSIG). As such, BDA was authorized by the Attorney General of New York to assist corporations with projects to ensure full compliance with State statutes. Accordingly, BDA has performed contract work for the Resolution Trust Company under FDIC approval. BDA is also a service member of the New York Bankers Association.

BDA's corporate clients range in size from international to small and midsize regional and local companies. BDA services clients from such business sectors as international and regional investment banking firms and banks, insurance companies, criminal and civil attorneys, retailers, and consumer product licensors and manufacturers. BDA also provides its services to individual clients, some of whom are high-net-worth and/or highly visible, celebrated individuals.

BDA's staff comprises a diversified group of highly skilled attorneys, certified public accountants, investigators, and certified fraud examiners with backgrounds in law enforcement, finance, commerce, and industry. Its legal staff includes former federal, state, and local law-enforcement officers, as well as corporate attorneys, with decades of combined experiences that span the spectrum of assignments. BDA's accomplished professionals bring extensive experience in domestic and international business to their assignments. The daily cross-disciplinary interaction among BDA staff members provides its clients with an unsurpassed scope of resources.

Notes

Chapter 1

Baltes, Sharon. "Dressing for Success Can be Puzzling But Rewarding." *Des Moines Business Record,* 12/6/04.

Bjorseth, Lillian. "Polish Your Appearance for Success," www.duoforce.com.

Chapter 2

Berlind, David. "Mixing Business and Pleasure." *Tech Update,* 12/2/03.

Bonne, Joan. "Are We Done With the 40-Hour Week?" MSNBC.com, 8/25/03.

Hecker, Daniel. "How Hours of Work Affect Occupational Earnings." *Monthly Labor Review,* 10/98, p. 8.

Ip, Greg. "U.S. Wealth Tied More to Work Than Productivity." *The Wall Street Journal*, 7/8/04, p. A2.

Chapter 3

Hart, Rupert. *Effective Networking for Professional Success* (Kogan Page, 1996).

Chapter 4

Hill, Napoleon. *Napoleon Hill's Keys to Success* (Dutton, 1994).

Chapter 5

Kalies, Bryon. *Across the Board*, August 2004, p. 5.
Yaverbaum, Eric, and Robert W. Bly. *Public Relations Kit for Dummies* (IDG).

Chapter 7

Bly, Robert. "Be a Better Bargainer." *Chemical Engineering Progress*, July 2002, pp. 91–92.

Chapter 8

Bly, Robert. "High Pay and High Risks for Contractors in Iraq." CNN.com, 4/1/04.

Ivanovich, David. "Silence Surrounds Fates of Contractors in Iraq." *Houston Chronicle*, 11/21/04.

Kelley, Matt. "U.S. Contractors in Iraq Fined." CNBCNEWS.com, 4/26/04.

Chapter 11

Kelley, Matt. "How to Motivate Your Employees," U.S. Small Business Administration Online Women's Business Center.

Yaverbaum, Eric. *Leadership Secrets of the World's Most Successful CEOs* (Dearborn, 2004).

Chapter 14

Bly, Robert. "A Firebrand at 69." *Writer's Digest*, May 2005.

McCormick, Jim. "Risking to Win." www.powerhomebiz.com.

Chapter 16

Lewinter, Howard. "CEOs Must Get Out of the Office."

Penttila, Chris. "Staff Overhaul." *Entrepreneur*, 9/01.

St. John, Warren. "Here Come the Glamour Gumshoes." *The New York Times*, 10/19/03.

Chapter 18

Bly, Robert W. *Doing the Right Thing: Ethics in the Workplace* (American Media Publishing, 1999).

Chapter 20

Bly, Robert. "Diamond Jim Brady: Porker." *Book of Lists*, p. 377; *Biography*, 8/03, p. 22.

———. "Malcolm Forbes, Capitalist." *The Washington Times*, 2/26/90.

Meldon, Jerry. "Our Man in Morocco." *IF* magazine, 10/99.

About the Authors

BO DIETL (www.beaudietl.com; 800-777-9366), having made more than 1,400 felony arrests during his fifteen years on the NYPD, "was probably the best detective in New York," according to Nicholas Pileggi, bestselling author of *Wiseguy.*

After retiring from the NYPD, Dietl founded Beau Dietl & Associates (BDA), one of the largest international companies specializing in corporate investigations and security.

Bo is a partner in several other business ventures, including One Tough Computer Cop, software that enables parents to monitor their children's activities on the Internet, and How Good Is This Production Company, a motion picture production company.

Films produced by How Good include *One Tough Cop, The Bone Collector, Table One, The Lucky Ones,* and *Jimmy the Wags.* Bo has also served as a consultant for numerous companies in motion pictures, television, and radio, including Sony, Columbia

Pictures, Universal, Lorimar Productions, Martin Bergman Productions, Westwood One, NBC, CBS, CNBC, CNN, and MSNBC.

BOB BLY (www.bly.com) is a freelance copywriter specializing in direct marketing and the author of more than sixty books. His articles have been published in *Cosmopolitan, Amtrak Express, New Jersey Monthly,* and *The Parent Paper.*

HOW TO BE A BETTER NEGOTIATOR

The conversations on business and networking between Bo Dietl and his friends were recorded in January 2005. In addition to the list of participants below, Bo would like to thank his good friends Marcy Simon, Sheldon Brody, and Admiral Robert Natter for their time and cooperation.

Ted Wait
Founder & Chairman
Gateway Computers

Jack Welch
Former Chairman & Chief Executive
    Officer
General Electric Company

Roger Enrico
Former Chairman & Chief Executive
    Officer of PepsiCo
Current Chairman of Dreamworks

John Myers
Chairman
General Electric Asset Management

Joseph Grano
Former Chairman & Chief Executive
    Officer of UBS PaineWebber
Current Chairman of Centurion
    Holdings LLC

Donny Deutsch
Chairman & Chief Executive Officer
Deutsch Advertising

Mark Arzoomanian
Chairman & Chief Executive Officer
Resources Search Company, Inc.

Bill O'Reilly
Correspondent/Show Host
FOX News Channel

Melvyn Weiss
Founder & General Partner
Milberg Weiss Bershad &
    Schulman LLP

Edward Straw
Former Chief Operating Officer of the
    Estée Lauder Companies
Retired 3-Star Admiral, U.S. Navy

Roger Ailes
Chairman & Chief Executive Officer
FOX News Channel

Steven Witkoff
Founder & Chairman
The Witkoff Group

Warren Buffet
Investment Icon